SPIRITUAL EXERCISES

Joining Body and Spirit in Prayer

NANCY ROTH

Seabury Books
an imprint of Church Publishing, Incorporated
New York, New York

A catalog record for this book is available from the Library of Congress.

ISBN 1-59627-005-5

Church Publishing, Incorporated
445 Fifth Avenue
New York, NY 10016

OTHER BOOKS BY NANCY ROTH

We Sing of God: A Hymnal for Children
Praying: A Book for Children
A Closer Walk: Meditating on Hymns for Year A
Awake My Soul! Meditating on Hymns for Year B
New Every Morning: Meditating on Hymns for Year C
Praise My Soul: Meditating on Hymns
The Breath of God: An Approach to Prayer
An Invitation to Christian Yoga (book and CD)
Organic Prayer
Meditations for Choir Members
Tween Prayer

Spiritual Exercises

TO MY TEACHERS OVER THE YEARS,

who have contributed so much to my
understanding of bodyspirit,
among them

*Agnes Hammerstrom, Angela Sartorio, Marguerite Duncan,
Carol Kelly, Leon Danielian, Maria Swoboda, Betty Goodman, Wendy Swallow,
Henry Danton, William Glassman, Eunice Wellington, Carla De Sola,
Mette Spaniardi, Liane Plane, Lee Brunner, Allegra Kent, Maralyn Miles, Finis Jhung,
Carol Hageman, Nancy Brenstuhl, Denise Gula, and Deborah Vogel.*

TABLE OF CONTENTS

ACKNOWLEDGMENTS

THANKS ARE DUE to Cynthia Crumlish, Bernice Goulden, and Deborah Vogel, who read and critiqued the entire manuscript, and to Richard Anderson, for his insights on the Alexander Technique. My husband Bob was, as always, my skilled and devoted first editor, and his support as I spent hours at the computer will never be forgotten. Finally, it is a joy and a privilege to work once again with Cynthia Shattuck and the other staff at Church Publishing.

A CONFESSION
TO ST. IGNATIUS

IF I WERE able to write a letter to St. Ignatius of Loyola, author of the original *Spiritual Exercises* published in 1535, it would go something like this.

Dear Ignatius,

I have a confession to make. I have stolen the title of your excellent book, *Spiritual Exercises.* Perhaps you will understand my motive if I offer an explanation.

Your book, written almost five hundred years ago, has served many people over the centuries, beginning with the order that you founded, the Society of Jesus. Your wisdom has guided many people. You propose a method of meditation and prayer that prepares the seeker for meaningful life, just as you once (before your conversion) prepared yourself for battle as a gallant soldier.

You would be amazed if you could travel through time to my century. Life is both the same and also very different now. People still seek deeper meaning for life. But our culture is not as conducive to that search as yours was. There is too much of everything: work, pleasure, information, worldly goods, stress, comfort—I could go on and on. So my friends in this century often struggle with a frustrating sense of fragmentation. We need to find our center.

Just as you have helped your readers find their center in prayer and meditation, I want to help my friends in this century find their center through experiencing the connection between their physical bodies and that unseen part of them that some call "spirit." My guess is that you, too, noted the connection between spiritual and physical exercise, because in the first paragraph of your book you wrote: "For just as strolling, walking, and running are bodily exercises, so spiritual exercises are methods of preparing and disposing the soul to free itself of all inordinate attachments, and after accomplishing this, of seeking and discovering the Divine Will regarding the disposition of one's life, thus insuring the salvation of his soul."

In my century, I would put it slightly differently. But I agree with you that spiritual exercises are not an end in themselves. Rather, whether they are your exercises or mine, they are a preparation for the fullness of a life in which we can contribute our gifts to a world in sore need, and in doing so, discover the joy of becoming better channels of the infinite love we call God.

Yours faithfully,

Nancy Roth

*

MARVELOUSLY MADE

I BEGIN WITH three vignettes.

I walk out the 42nd Street exit from Manhattan's Grand Central Terminal and am greeted by a sight I have never seen during all my years in New York: people are actually staring at someone. Those familiar with the city know that rarely does an unusual sight attract attention. Passers-by live up to their name, ignoring various states of dress and undress, odd behavior, and manic sidewalk preaching. This is different.

Slowly but surely, a Buddhist monk dressed in saffron robes is making his way east along the sidewalk. His eyes are cast down, and he holds a begging bowl. He moves at a snail's pace, placing one foot after the other deliberately, as if the bowl he holds were the whole weight of the fragile earth borne in his hands. However, it is not the sight of the monk that draws attention. It is his quality of movement. That quality generates what can be best described by the word "aura," like the golden halos around the saints in medieval paintings. It is not visible to the eye, but it is certainly apparent to the crowd on the sidewalk. It radiates calm and grounded-ness. The monk is more *there* than anyone else on the sidewalk, and frenetic New Yorkers recognize it and pause to pay homage. I assume he is undertaking a peace walk from the United Nations headquarters on the east end of 42nd Street to the western end of that busy thoroughfare. But his primary task is the doing, rather than the destination. He will remain in my memory, garbed in the color of daybreak and placing one foot after another, a symbol of the hope that peaceful presence can bring to our chaotic world.

I am at a conference, where a professor of historical theology from Harvard Divinity School is about to make a presentation. She follows some quite heady academics who have read lectures that were thought-provoking at the time, but that I have long since forgotten. She tells us that our concept of our bodies is formed by the images that surround us. The lights go out, and slides begin to appear on the screen behind her. Look, she tells us, this is what informed our ancestors about their bodies. We see photos of early Christian paintings on the walls of the catacombs: Jesus and the saints, praying with upraised hands. We see stylized icons, understood by those who venerate them as windows to eternity. We see increasingly three-dimensional paintings and sculptures from the Middle Ages and early Renaissance, picturing people who derived their value from who they were and their relationships with one another, rather than from how they appeared. The silent messages proclaimed by these images seeped into our ancestors' unconscious, although they were not aware of it.

Now, she says to us, by what images are *you* surrounded? On the screen there appear pictures from the world of marketing: glossy magazine photos meant to tempt us to buy their wares. The bodies are thin. They are white. They are young.

What does this do to you? she asks. These pictures seep into your unconscious. They are meant to disturb you, to make you unhappy with your body. They are sending the message that if you buy this perfume, that brand of Scotch, or these shoes, you will look like us. But most of us are not as thin as these models, and none of us can remain young, and many of us are not white. The result is that, in our culture, dissatisfaction with our bodies is an epidemic. A new model of the body needs to be offered.

✳

I am giving a workshop. I call it "Spiritual Exercises." Some of the participants are fit; they have incorporated exercise into their schedules. A few of them regret not being equally devoted to their interior lives.

Others have allowed the demands of their jobs to crowd out adequate concern for their physical well-being. There is not time, they say. I expend all my energy on giving to others. I find time to pray, but it is impossible to fit an exercise program into my daily life.

I am offering a smorgasbord to you, I tell them. It is a smorgasbord of practices that can help you integrate your physical health and your spiritual practice. All will help you become more aware of your bodies as "temples" of God's Spirit, motivating you to become better stewards of your time, of your body, and of your spirit.

From this smorgasbord you can choose to incorporate into your daily life those practices that most appeal to you. Maybe it will simply be paying closer attention to your breathing and your posture. You may find exercises from hatha yoga, tai chi, Pilates, or Alexander Techniques congenial. You may discover new connections between your physical and spiritual well-being through dance, walking, strength training, aerobic exercise, or even the daily exercise that you do as you go about the chores of maintaining a house or garden.

On the dessert table are some further choices. They are suggestions about how movement can *become* prayer: contemplative, reflective, and verbal. You might even begin to experience rest and relaxation as a kind of body-prayer.

You will not have to make an effort to think much in this workshop, because you will let your body do the thinking for you. There is wisdom encoded in your physical self, just as there is in all the created order made by God. Learn from your bodies, God's temples here on earth.

We finish the workshop. Is there a book about this? I am asked. Not yet, I have to admit.

Finally, here it is.

*

The vignettes you have just read suggest the themes in this book. The image of the monk remains with me as an example of someone whose spiritual practice integrated body and spirit: he was a living demonstration of the fact that the words "wholeness" and "holiness" come from the same Anglo-Saxon root. The Harvard professor affirmed my growing awareness of the need to think in new ways about the role of the body in Christian spirituality. The response to my workshops and retreats on this subject reveals the increasing hunger among people to integrate physical life with the life of the spirit.

This integration has not always been one of the goals of Christian spirituality. When I was in my twenties, I subscribed to the Library of St. Bede, a lending library of religious classics based at the Church of the Resurrection in New York City. I regularly chose from their bibliography those books that promised to satisfy my growing inquisitiveness about the life of the spirit. Many of these books were the work of the mystics of the church; some of them were textbooks in ascetical theology dating from the early years of the twentieth century. It was quickly apparent that the attitude of the great majority of writers was that the body was an impediment, and needed to be disciplined so that the Christian could escape its constraints.

At the same time, I was studying ballet seriously, and had just become a mother. I had discovered that the focused discipline of a ballet class calmed and centered my spirit while it strengthened and stretched my body. I had trusted my body to take me safely through the rhythms of childbirth. My body did not feel like an impediment, but like an instrument—for a beautiful art, and for giving life and then nurturing it.

The moment of truth occurred one Ash Wednesday, when I was determined to fast all day long, as was my custom. Although fasting has an appropriate place in the spiritual practices of many people, it apparently is not suitable for someone with my metabolism. I remember becoming so weak that all I could do was lie on the sofa in the baby's room, until common sense got the better of me. Surely God intended me to be strong in body so that I could care for my child. I began to wonder if those things that gave me a sense of strength and well-being, like a healthful diet, exercise, and proper rest, were not better suited to modern Christian spirituality. They certainly worked better for me.

Seminary gave me an intellectual context in which to explore this issue theologically, and provided a forum in which to begin teaching what I had learned. I had taken some hatha yoga classes and realized that they were an ideal way to quiet my spirit and prepare for prayer, so I developed Christian yoga classes for my classmates at General Seminary, and, later, for the seekers who came to weekday programs at Trinity Church, Wall Street. I met a fellow explorer who was doing the same thing with tai chi, and we shared our disciplines. I gathered material through liturgical dance workshops and classes in many disciplines, and I invented some of my own.

I begin this book by setting the stage, suggesting an attitude toward the body that is deeply rooted in a biblical understanding of the body as a sacred space, brought to life and sustained by the breath of our Creator. We will consider what that means in various periods of our lives, from childhood through old age. Like our medieval ancestors, who believed that God's revelation comes to us through two sources, the Book of Scripture and the Book of Nature, we will learn to read our most familiar part of the Book of Nature—our physical bodies—in terms of metaphor. What does the structure of our foot, or the center of our physical equilibrium, or the invigorating renewal of aerobic exercise, tell us about God's presence with us and our response to it?

Onto the stage I will then bring a revue: a series of ways in which to engage your body as a partner in your spiritual path. It is very likely that you will resonate to some disciplines more than to others. That is the point in offering variety: we are all different. I suggest that you take what you like best and pursue it, through classes, videotapes, or books.

Above all, I hope this book will enable you to become aware of your body as a worthy partner in your journey with God, not just at the time of practicing the disciplines you have chosen, but in every moment of daily life.

I will thank you because I am marvelously made;
* your works are wonderful, and I know it well.*
My body was not hidden from you,
* while I was being made in secret*
*   and woven in the depths of the earth.*

Your eyes beheld my limbs, yet unfinished in the womb;
  all of them were written in your book;
    they were fashioned day by day,
  when as yet there was none of them.
How deep I find your thoughts, O God!
  how great is the sum of them!

(Psalm 139:13–16)[1]

CHAPTER 1

FULLY ALIVE

IN THE CENTER of the children's playground near my grandson's Brooklyn home is an array of sprinklers, activated when the summer temperature begins to rise. Gabriel noticed these when I took him to the park on one of the first days they made their seasonal debut. Secretly wishing I could have run through the mist myself, I removed his shoes but not his clothes, thinking that, at fourteen months, he might be somewhat cautious about this new experience. Wrong! He toddled up to one of the fountains, squinched up his face when the water hit it, then broke into gales of laughter: "Water! Water!" A few steps forward, and he was surrounded by the mist, turning and laughing "Water! Water!"—the picture of joy. I couldn't decide if he reminded me more of a dancing Hassidic Jew or the famous Bernini statue of St. Teresa in ecstasy.

Gabriel, so fully alive both in body and in spirit, reminded me of the pleasure of my childhood summers at the beach, when my brothers and I adopted the Atlantic Ocean as our favorite playmate. But even at home in our suburban neighborhood, physical play filled the long hours that many children now spend sitting in front of television sets or computer screens. I have often been grateful that I grew up before video monitors replaced playing tag or hide-and-seek, hopscotch, skipping rope, or riding bikes as a way to spend a long summer afternoon.

My most sedentary period of life occurred during high school, when I was a perfectionist student and avid pianist, practicing long hours every afternoon and often studying long into the night. I distinctly remember my frequent fatigue during those years. On coming home from school, I would sometimes fall asleep in the chair opposite the front door before I even took off my coat.

I had taken creative movement and ballet classes in elementary school, but had chosen "social" dancing instead when I was twelve because it involved boys. But ballet had been imprinted in my soul, and, after an eight-year hiatus in adolescence, I longed to go back. I bravely tried a couple of classes in Paris where I studied during my junior year of college, and enrolled in the Ballet Russe de Monte Carlo school in New York the following summer.

It was difficult to get started again. I knew what my body was supposed to do, but it felt as though the neurological pathways from my brain to my muscles had to be re-cleared, like an old mountain road filled with the debris of long years of neglect. As I persevered, I rediscovered what I knew so well in childhood: I didn't merely *have* a body, with its inconvenient needs for rest or nourishment that interrupted my real work. I *was* a body.

Having once again begun ballet classes at the age of twenty, I have never stopped since. The classic discipline of ballet was a language programmed into my body in my childhood, and it is one of the ways I still experience being fully alive.

By the time I became pregnant with our first child, I had enough faith in my body to tell my family doctor that I wanted natural childbirth, in an era when it was still a rarity. I took ballet classes right up to my due date, had an easy labor, and cherish that birth, as well as the birth of our second son, as a high point in my life.

At about the same time I began to reclaim the physical part of my nature, I discovered something more about the spiritual part as well. I had been a devout teenager, fervent about both the ritual and the rules of the church in which I grew up. I was exposed to a more personal approach to God when I began to read the writings of the mystics. I had always had the sense that the physical reality I could see and touch was a "thin" place, and that there was a spirit both deeper and closer that pervaded all things, but I had never found words to express this intuition. The language of the mystics gave voice to what I could not say:

He is our clothing. In his love he wraps and holds us.
He enfolds us for love, and he will never let us go. *(Julian of Norwich)*

On a dark night,
Kindled in love with yearnings—oh, happy chance!...
My face I reclined on the Beloved.
All ceased and I abandoned myself,
Leaving my cares forgotten among the lilies. *(John of the Cross)*

I began to think of the soul as if it were a castle made of a single diamond or
of very clear crystal, in which there are many rooms. *(Teresa of Avila)*

Mystics such as these convinced me that poetry and metaphor are the best language
in which to express the experience of the holy. Meeting the mystics through literature certainly inspired my own life work of helping others to experience the presence and love of God through teaching and writing.

As I enter the final third of my life, there is a metaphor from Scripture that increasingly appeals to me. It occurs in the letters of St. Paul to the young (and, we can guess,
rather unruly) congregation in Corinth. "Do you not know that your body is a temple of the Holy Spirit within you, which you have from God, and that you are not
your own?... Therefore glorify God in your body."

Speaking to a congregation today, Paul would probably use the word "cathedral"
or "church" instead of temple to convey the idea of holy space. We are "cathedrals,"
like the great English cathedrals my husband and I have visited over the years, along
with thousands of other pilgrims and tourists. They are holy spaces, not because of
some magical formula that makes them so, but because of all the life and worship that
has happened within them. Those who are sensitive to such things insist that, especially in those moments in the late afternoon or early mornings when the tourists are
gone, the air is so thick with prayer that you can cut it with a knife.

The buildings that contain all this holiness show their age. No one would dare suggest that the stairs worn concave by the feet of centuries of pilgrims climbing to
Thomas à Becket's former shrine in Canterbury or by the feet of clerics wending
their way to a meeting in the Chapter House at Wells ought to be made level for purposes of esthetics or even safety. Most of these buildings are well cared for. Alms boxes
accepting financial contributions toward building maintenance welcome visitors, and

scaffolding is the norm rather than the exception. But no one ever tries to make these places look new again. Their beauty lies in the signs of a long life—the worn steps, the occasional missing pieces in the stained glass or chips off the woodcarvings, the moss and small plants growing on the walls. The more I understand myself as a temple or cathedral, the less I worry about the outward signs of aging, aside from doing my best to maintain my health, strength, and flexibility. The metaphor helps me to celebrate the fact that, contrary to the opinions of the youth-worshiping culture in which we live, every era of life has its own beauty. It reminds me that the longer I live, the more time I am given to fill this holy space with the life-spirit that is the gift of God.

As I look back over the years, I see that there are several ways I could write my autobiography. One is about myself as "earth"—bones, organs, muscles, ligaments, skin, and all the rest. Another is about myself as "spirit," because I have been the recipient of the gift of life, a fact of which I am reminded every time I draw breath. This gift is from outside me; I cannot generate it myself. I experience the Giver as that Otherness of whom the mystics spoke so clearly to me: the One who wraps and holds me in love, the Beloved for whom I yearn, the Dweller within the castle that is my soul. Best of all, however, is the autobiography in which I recognize I am both earth and spirit, for it is, in fact, artificial to even try to separate them. That is why, long ago, I eliminated the "and" when I wrote about body and spirit. The resulting word "bodyspirit" confused my publisher's spell-checkers—until they adjusted.

Before you continue reading, I invite you to close this book and reflect on your own autobiography, remembering moments in which you have been most aware of the physical aspects of the human condition.

Recall the childhood activities that made you feel vibrantly happy and alive, and the times in adolescence or adulthood in which you were both most aware and least aware of your body.

Recall the "spirit" part of your life. What writers and teachers have influenced you? What experiences shaped you? Have religious institutions played a part, or has it been your own private, personal journey?

When have you best known the integration of both the earth and spirit aspects of yourself? Have there been moments when, above all, you experienced yourself not as divided but as a unity of bodyspirit, fully alive?

Becoming more fully alive and regarding our bodies as holy spaces are both ways of describing a particular theological attitude toward the human condition. Such an attitude has implications for our spiritual practices. One of the things that greatly puzzled me when I was studying the lives of some of the early saints and medieval mystics of the Christian tradition was what seemed to me to be their skewed idea of the body. I wondered what gave Simeon Stylites the notion that it would be pleasing to God to live, immobile, on top of a sixty-foot pillar for years, although it was reported that from that perch he "converted many pagans and awakened the careless." Why did the flagellants of the thirteenth and fourteenth centuries process across Europe, all the while whipping their own backs until they were bloodied? More shockingly, why did self-flagellation continue to be a required spiritual discipline in some religious orders even within my own lifetime? How, during all these centuries, particularly in the context of the Christian faith that preaches the Incarnation, could the body have been considered an enemy, to be tamed and broken like an unruly colt? Did these punishing practices truly help people to live as Jesus—who, according to the gospel narratives, enjoyed good food, good wine, and good company—would have them live?

Needless to say, it is easy to err in the opposite direction. Self-indulgence is not any more helpful to the journey of faith than is self-punishment. But true discipline, in the name of health, wholeness, and holiness, begins with appreciation of this wonder that is our physical being. *I will thank you, because I am marvelously made.*

The word "asceticism" is derived from the Greek word for exercise, or training. In my experience, there are abundant opportunities to practice asceticism in this sense. They happen when we are tempted to avoid things that we know would benefit our physical and spiritual health. *Not* going out for our daily walk, for example, because sitting in front of the television or the computer is so very seductive: "Why should I bother?" *Not* taking the exercise class for which I have signed up: "Today I'm just too busy." After years of trial and error, I can attest to the fact that the times when I feel least like subjecting myself to the effort of a ballet class are the times when I need most to go, for afterward I am revived, with the ability to sleep especially soundly that night!

Opportunities also present themselves when we are tempted to do things that we know might damage our health, like overeating. These opportunities often occur in the kitchen or in restaurants, and are made more complicated by the fact that many of us use food for comforting ourselves, rather than eating because we are hungry. The reasons for obesity are, of course, complex, and advice is readily available from both medical and psychological sources. Suffice it to say that, as with all care of self, our approach to eating is a prime example of the bodyspirit connection. A friend once accomplished the extraordinary feat of losing ninety pounds in a year, after years of trying to manage her weight. What made the difference? Her success was due to a journal she kept: "Not a food diary, but a journal in which I discussed with myself those things that were bothering me."

This brand of asceticism can be demanding: it takes guts to say "no" to our bodies when they crave a second serving of chocolate cake or a third martini or a cigarette. But every time we can say "no," we are becoming freer people—stewards of our bodies, rather than slaves of our bodies.

This theology is articulated in a prayer said for the blessing of a home, as the priest and family gather at the door of the bathroom:

> O holy God, in the incarnation of your Son our Lord you made our flesh the instrument of your self-revelation: Give us a proper respect and reverence for our mortal bodies, keeping them clean and fair, whole and sound...glorifying you in them.[2]

Even during the periods of outrageously negative attitudes toward the body, the liturgy itself was suggesting this message. Worship was not merely an intellectual exercise, but a physical one. Small children were brought to the font to be baptized with water. Worshipers were given the bread of the Eucharist. The ill were anointed with holy oil. The dead were lovingly buried with prayer.

As we move into the twenty-first century, it is especially urgent that we reclaim our concept of self as bodyspirit. I know that my own understanding of myself as part of the web of life on earth has made me more aware of my connection both with the natural world and with all other human beings. I cannot view with detachment either the media images of someone afflicted by the violence of war or of old growth forest laid bare by clear-cutting. This view of the human being as bodyspirit has an effect not only on my prayer, but on my action in the world, shaping not only my political views but also the way I shop, cook, and garden. This way of looking at our human condition and its place in the world leads to transformation.

It is also cause for celebration, because we need not look only within the walls of the religious institution for holiness and wholeness: our bodies themselves can teach us. In them is revealed, if we have eyes to see and ears to hear, the wisdom of our Creator. Our bodies are, like all of nature and the great scriptures of the faith traditions, books about God. I finally put a name to this insight, as I sat one day in a class called "Body Reeducation and Alignment," a course for dancers and theater majors at Oberlin College. Our teacher, Deborah Vogel, had worked in New York with injured dancers and actors who came to her when the medical professionals had thrown up their hands in despair. She can read the body like an X-ray machine, and knows better than anyone I have ever met how it is meant to function. During each class, as she uncovered the mysteries of the way we ought to stand, walk, sit, and dance, I found myself making connections. Why does proper breathing, whether of oxygen or of God's life-giving Spirit, give us vitality? How does the way I stand affect my sense of emotional stability? Can shedding muscular tension help me to shed grievances? The answers to these questions beckon us into the realm of prayer, faith, and forgiveness. What works for my body, I realized in this class, is also what works for my spirit. It was, I decided, a class in "kinetic theology."

*

CHAPTER 2

SPIRITUAL EXERCISES

ONE OF THE common complaints of people who come to me for counseling is that they cannot fit into their crowded lives all the activities they wish they could do. The demands of work, home, and family often consume so much time that attention to their body's health or their spirit's refreshment gets short shrift. One way of moving toward a solution, I believe, is to expand our concept of prayer.

Many people consider prayer to be something set apart from the demands of their daily schedule, perhaps early in the morning or before going to bed. People who set apart such time can testify to the profound impact of this practice on their sense of God's presence with them throughout each day. For that reason, such regular, intentional prayer can be described as *practice* for remembering that God is with us in every moment, no matter what we are doing.

Spiritual teachers speak of this kind of remembering as "recollection." I like that word, because it implies that we are bringing together something that had been fragmented, the way we would pick up a child's wooden puzzle that had tumbled to the floor in order to put the pieces back together again. In this case, the pieces are daily life and prayer—"body" and "spirit." When we put those two pieces together, they describe our humanity, one bodyspirit. We are bodyspirit in all our activities, and that includes the exercise that we do, whether it be on machines at the gym, behind lawn-mowers, on bicycles, or in the water.

When I first heard the words of Paul, "Pray without ceasing," as a child, I thought that it meant going through life perpetually mumbling a prayer. While, in fact, there is a prayer practice that involves constant repetition of a phrase (you will read about it later), I eventually realized that praying without ceasing is really "recollection." It is awareness, sometimes in our conscious minds and sometimes so habitual that we do not even think about it, that God is within us and with us. If you have known intense love—of a partner, a spouse, a child, or a grandchild—you know what I mean. We carry the relationship within us constantly. Perhaps that is why the language of the mystics is often so similar to love poetry.

If we are bodyspirit, and if God is with us in all things, that means that physical exercise can be an integral part of our recollection and prayer. The things we do for the sake of our body's well-being can also nourish our relationship with God.

In the following pages I have given you some examples, drawing from the disciplines with which I have some familiarity. Obviously, I do not have space to present any one discipline in great depth. Instead, I try to convey the essence of each form of exercise by providing a few examples of each so that you can experience its spirit for yourself. If I have omitted a form of exercise you practice, I urge you to explore ways in which it also can be part of your prayer.

BREATHING

Breathing is involuntary, continuing day and night, and absolutely necessary to our life. The cells of our body acquire their energy not only through the nutrients we eat but through the constant supply of oxygen our breathing provides. After we inhale, the oxygen rides on the back of hemoglobin in our blood until it reaches the tiny thin-walled capillaries, where it is provided to the tissue and exchanged for carbon dioxide. The deoxygenated blood then flows back through the veins, traveling into larger and larger blood vessels until it reaches the heart. There, it is once again pumped out to the lungs to receive new oxygen. If this process stops for too long, the cells of our bodies starve, our brains stop functioning, and we die. The Psalmist knew that well as he meditated on the manifold creatures who dwell on the wondrous earth: "You take away their breath, and they die and return to their dust" (Ps.104:30).

While we do not have choice—at least until our last moments on earth—about whether or not to breathe, we do have the capacity to increase the efficiency of our breath. A healthy lung is capable of inhaling more than a gallon of air. Under average conditions, we inhale only about a pint of air with each breath. This may be sufficient when we are resting, but when more energy is required of us, whether it be to go on a long hike or to sprint to catch a train, it is necessary to use more of our breathing apparatus. To learn how we can do this, it is helpful to know some physiology.

We all know that we have two lungs, but did you know that the left one is smaller than the right, because it must share space in the chest with the heart and part of the stomach? (This explains why it is sometimes hard to breathe properly after an enormous meal.) The lungs, which have no muscles, are like a viscous liquid, expanding into any empty space with which they are in contact. This empty space is provided by the movement of our muscles.

There are two groups of respiratory muscles. The most powerful of the primary muscles is the diaphragm, which is intended to do the bulk of the work. It lies below the lungs and is shaped like a vaulted sheath. It is sometimes likened to a parachute, not only because of its capacity to expand, but because its fibers, like the strings of a parachute, attach to vertebrae in the lumbar spine (the small of the back), the end of the breastbone, and some of the ribs. The diaphragm is assisted by the other primary muscles—the *intercostals* between the ribs, and the *abdominal* muscles that girdle the front of the belly.

The secondary muscles are higher up in the body. They are the thin *scalenus* in the front of the neck, which attach to the uppermost ribs; the *pectoralis* in the chest, so prominent in body-builders; the *sternocleidomastoid*, running from just behind the ear to the top of the sternum and clavicle; and the *upper trapezius*, which run from the base of the skull to the top of the shoulder blades. These secondary muscles are generally smaller and more delicate, tiring easily. Their role is to lift the ribs up to make room for more oxygen; they can act efficiently for short periods of time when we need short bursts of extra energy. Physiologists warn us never to reverse the roles by asking these secondary muscles to do the work of the diaphragm and the other primary muscles. The secondary breathing muscles can never become what they were not intended to be: prime movers of the oxygen to and from our lungs.

When we were infants, we all breathed fully and naturally. During his first months of life, when our grandson lay on his back in his crib, his relaxed breath moved his entire belly, because it was primarily his diaphragm that was working. However, when he became upset—because of colic, hunger, or even fatigue—he would "wind up" with a long deep breath, while we held *our* breath—and sometimes our ears—because we knew what was coming: a long piercing scream, his only way of communicating discomfort. I could picture all those muscles, from the diaphragm on up to the upper trapezius, making room during those "wind up" moments for his lungs to fill with air in order to reach peak volume.

Were I to ask a group of ten people to take a deep breath, I would probably see nine out of ten pairs of shoulders rising, rather than the in-and-out movement of the belly and ribcage. Most adults have forgotten the free and relaxed breathing that came so naturally to us as infants. This is often due to fashion, such as tight clothes that constrain the pelvis, or to posture, like slumping over a computer keyboard. To learn to breathe properly is mainly a matter of shedding the bad habits that prevent us from breathing like babies, with what Donna Farhi calls the "essential breath" of infancy:

> When you were born your whole body breathed. Every cell quivered with the vitality of the breath. Every bone, muscle, and organ moved with every breath. Every nerve was energized by it, every blood cell carried it, and every moment took as its meter the phrasing of your breath. Today, most of us have forgotten what it feels like to breathe fully and wholly with the vitality of the newborn infant. We have forgotten this but we have not lost it. In reclaiming the fullness of our breathing we also reclaim many other dimensions of our lives.[3]

Ideally, we should not consciously control the way we breathe by either deliberately slowing it down or speeding it up. But relearning that "essential breath" takes some practice. (Donna Farhi calls her book on breathing a "how-to-undo" book.) Paradoxically, free breathing is a result of deep relaxation, not of effort. In order to "undo," we need to rediscover some of those primary and secondary muscles that allow our lungs to expand and contract, and teach them to relax and to move.

Lie on your back with the knees bent and the feet flat on the floor. Close your eyes, and mentally scan your entire body, letting it relax and sink into the floor. Then begin to focus gently on the area below your navel. Tense the muscles inward and notice how that feels. Then release the tension and notice how relaxation feels. Now, keeping the muscles relaxed, notice the natural movement of the abdomen as you breathe. Notice that the lower part of the torso billows outward in all directions as you inhale: up, toward your sides, and into your back. The fact is that although we do not "breathe" with the abdomen, unless we relax it as we breathe, the diaphragm cannot fully expand.

Do you feel the ribs—front, sides, and back—expanding and contracting like a bellows?

Is there movement in the pelvic floor—the bottom of the torso—as you breathe in and out?

Do you notice that, with each inhalation, the small of the back (lumbar spine) gently curves away from the floor, and with each exhalation, it relaxes down toward the floor?

Now focus on the subtle movement of the spinal column, imagining that the vertebrae of the spine are the fronds of a fern-like seaweed, floating up and down as the wave of your breath passes through the body.

If you now place your hands against the side of the hip bones, you will feel a subtle outward "breathing" motion of the hips as the bones of the pelvis rotate slightly at each inhalation.

These small movements, like a gentle swell in the ocean, are caused by breathing in such a way that these lower areas of the body open and release fully. Do not try to make them happen: just notice if they do happen. As you become more flexible and more in touch with your body, these movements will come naturally.

Now stand, and bring your attention to your shoulders. Inhale, and see if you can feel the way the inhalation expands the shoulders away from the center of the body. Your arms also will rotate slightly outward, away from the center, as you inhale and rotate inward as you exhale.

Next, either standing or lying down again, picture your skin as a knitted sheath that covers the entire body. As you inhale, imagine the strands of the sheath stretching, as they expand in order to create space for the breathing body. As you exhale, imagine the strands retracting and the fiber becoming denser. Enjoy the feeling of the whole body swelling and subsiding.

As you inhale and exhale, do you notice a slight pause before you begin to inhale again? That is an important pause, marking the borderline in the exchange of carbon dioxide for new oxygen.

Standing, cup your hands slightly, and begin to tap on your upper chest with both hands. Cover as much of the area of the chest as you can. Now ask someone else to cup their hands and do the same thing over the surface of your back. Does your breathing feel freer now? A nurse friend tells me that this is what she does for patients who have congestion in their lungs, but even healthy lungs can benefit.

As you continue to turn the pages of this book, you will discover many other ways, such as the stretching of hatha yoga or the cardiovascular activity of aerobic exercise, to increase your breathing capacity and to allow the "essential breath" to come naturally. When I took up ballet classes again in my early twenties, for example, I discovered that my ability to sing improved. I had been a member of the teenage choir at church when I was in high school, and sometimes felt a constriction in my throat as well as a lack of breath during rehearsals and services. The dramatic change when I began to exercise again happened because physical activity had called upon my lungs to work much harder than they had during those sedentary high school years. It showed me that I breathe not only with my lungs, but with my whole body.

Breathing has always been such a rich image for me that I entitled my first book *The Breath of God*,[4] an approach to prayer based on this essential function of our bodies. Just as breathing, which comes so naturally, is essential for our physical life, "breathing in" God in prayer is also a natural part of what it means to be human, and is equally essential for our spirits—itself a breath-word! I habitually connect my prayer with breathing, and the reverse can be true, as well: attention to my breathing reminds me of God's presence with me.

The oxygen of God's presence is calming, strengthening, and reassuring. The week after I had discussed this integration of breath and prayer with a class in Manhattan, one of the participants came to class with a testimonial: "I was on the subway, and the crowded train stopped between stations. The lights went out and I began to feel panicky. Then I decided to *breathe.* Do you know what? It works!" Another participant told of being in an elevator that became stuck between floors in a high-rise; she took the opportunity to teach the other trapped occupants about breathing to release tension, calming everybody down until a mechanic came to free them.

It is no wonder that breathing is one of the primary tools in calming and relaxing our minds. When we breathe our gratitude to God for the gift of life, our inhalation and exhalation renew every cell of our bodies. More than that, our breathing renews our spirits, too, helping us to become more and more fully alive.

WALKING

Probably the only people who do not take walking for granted are the very young, the very old, and those with an injury, such as a broken ankle, or a debilitating illness, like arthritis.

Consider the difficulties of the first year of life. During our grandson's first summer, my husband and I witnessed his utter frustration as he struggled to lift his stout little stomach off the floor in order to crawl. Once this was finally accomplished, he had to figure out how to coordinate moving forward. Finally, one day, he pulled himself up to a standing position. He decided that he liked seeing the world from this new perspective, and soon discovered that he could edge sideways by holding on to convenient furniture, like a passenger moving along the ship's railing in a gale. Once in a while, he dared to let go and stood proudly for a second or two on his own, as the grownups applauded. Finally, lured by the babysitter's cell-phone held a few feet out of reach, he took his first steps, and the telephones began to ring in the homes of grandparents, aunts, and uncles. If Gabriel becomes a student of anatomy someday, he will learn that each step he takes requires the cooperation of no fewer than two hundred muscles in his small body. Walking is no small accomplishment.

At the other end of the spectrum, around the retirement community at the edge of our town there is a well-used sidewalk where residents can get some outdoor exercise by walking the periphery of the campus. The observer notices a variety of gaits, from the athletic to the arthritic. However, not all the residents can walk: indoors, the electric wheelchairs parked outside the dining room bring to mind the local supermarket parking lot. Locomotion, whether independent, assisted by a cane or a walker, or dependent on the use of a wheelchair, is never taken for granted there.

One need not be struggling to walk in order to appreciate the ability to do so. In my class on anatomy for dance majors, I marveled when the professor began to describe the foot as a complex design of no less than twenty-six bones connected by muscles and ligaments. She explained that the arches in the foot make it strong because of their ability to bear stress and counter-stress. "A Gothic cathedral!," I thought, and pictured myself walking around on miniature Notre Dames or Westminster Abbeys.

Walking as spiritual exercise begins with gratitude for our ability to walk. There are several ways to use this simple movement as part of our prayer, through some of the following exercises.

Discovering the Feet. Take off your shoes and massage the feet to waken and warm them. Massage the soles, then spread out the toes and massage each one. Stretch and massage the top of the foot between the metatarsal bones, stroking toward each toe.

Stand and notice your weight entering the ground. Align your body so that your ears are over your shoulders, your shoulders are over your hipbones, and your hipbones are over the center of your foot where it bends at the ankle. Your weight should be distributed equally among the three points of a "tripod": the pads of the little toe, the big toe, and the heel. I have always found that it helps to picture my body as a skeleton in a biology classroom, hanging from a loop attached to the center of my skull. That image helps my bones just relax into place. The imaginary loop at the top of my skull is holding me erect by pulling me upward, while the force of gravity pulls my bones naturally toward the earth. When I stand like this, my lungs can fill with deep breaths.

This simple posture is itself a "spiritual exercise." Just standing in this way helps me remember that I belong here. I am drawn to the earth, my present home, by the force of gravity. In Brian Swimme's *The Universe is a Green Dragon,* an imaginary conversation with theologian Thomas Berry, the author proposes that gravity is one of the many forms of "allurement," or love, that holds the cosmos together. We are literally *drawn* toward this planet, rather than spinning off into space. The simple act of experiencing gravity as a metaphor for our earthliness reminds me of the gift of life here.

At the same time, our bodies have evolved to stand erect, rather than to respond to gravity by crumpling to the floor. We are not merely creatures of earth. Our ancestors, who pictured God as "up there," would say that standing erect is a metaphor for the fact that we are also creatures who are meant to reach toward God. We live in the tension between these two poles. We are both preoccupied with the exigencies of life on earth and yearning for the eternal.

Knowing where we stand—between earth and heaven—and actually *standing* there helps keep us grounded physically, emotionally, and spiritually. Standing like this is a good exercise to practice when we find ourselves waiting in line at the supermarket or post office. It can become a prayer of gratitude for life, offered to God, who has been called the Ground of our Being. And it readies us to move forward.

Unlike the Gothic cathedrals, our feet are designed to *move*. I remember going barefoot during the long summers of my childhood, feeling the textures of grass, mud, and pebbles against the soles of my feet, playing at picking up things with my toes. For most of us, modern life and confining footwear give us few opportunities for that kind of freedom. In the interests of both the health and the efficiency of our feet, we need to rediscover their amazing capabilities.

Turn your attention to your feet again. Stand and spread out your toes, as if you were imitating a duck with webbed feet. Press one toe at a time into the floor, as if you were trying to play scales on a piano. Flex the toes upward.

Press the toes flat against the floor, so that the metatarsal arch (the arch that goes across the foot directly behind the toes) rises. You can activate this arch in other ways as well, such as trying to pick up a marble with your toes, or pleating a towel with your toes. Because we use this arch so seldom, do not be surprised if you get a cramp: simply flex the toes, and it will go away.

With your feet flat on the floor again, roll the weight to the outside of the feet, then to the inside. Now center your weight firmly on the feet, keeping the weight distributed equally among the three points of the tripod of little toe, big toe, and heel.

Rise on your toes, then lower the feet. Now bend the knees to stretch the Achilles tendon behind the ankle.

Sit in a chair and flex the feet upward, then point them downward.

Remaining seated, circle each foot at the ankle, clockwise and counterclockwise.

Do your feet feel more alive after these exercises?

Meditation Walking

Meditation walking as a spiritual practice began in the Buddhist tradition. When the Buddha was asked, "What do you and your disciples practice?" he replied, "We sit, we walk, and we eat." When the questioner continued, "But, sir, everyone sits, walks, and eats," he responded, "When we sit, we know we are sitting. When we walk, we know we are walking. When we eat, we know we are eating."[5] Walking meditation is an expression of *apranihita,* or wishlessness. Walking is not a means to an end; walking is done for the sake of walking.

When I look for appearances of walking meditation in the history of western spirituality, I think immediately of the cloister—a covered walk with an open colonnade on one side, running along a quadrangle of buildings—attached to so many European cathedrals and abbeys. In my mind's eye I see monks walking through the cloister, rain or shine, pondering Scripture, and, I would hope, enjoying the sight of the herb and flower gardens in the center. Or perhaps, after long hours sitting in cell or chapel and aching for exercise, they were simply walking for the sake of walking! Whatever their motivation, certainly they also were practicing the mindfulness sought by their Buddhist brothers far away.

In teaching mindful walking, I have found it helpful to break down the physical action of putting one foot in front of the other slowly and deliberately. If you were to take a movie of someone walking "normally" and then slow the speed at which you project it on the screen, you would be surprised to discover that the way we usually walk involves losing our balance over and over again, as we literally "fall" from foot to foot. In meditation walking, on the other hand, we never "fall." Instead, we slowly place our weight on each foot in turn. People who try this for the first time find out that balance is a challenge.

Meditation walking can be done anywhere there is room to move and where you can find a sense of relative privacy and quiet. You may have a house like mine, where each room opens into the next, and you can walk in a circular path. Or you may have a few square feet in your living room or study. Perhaps there is a secluded corner in your backyard, or a quiet area in a nearby park. A church—either the worship space when it is not in use or a large empty room used for gatherings—serves this purpose well. If you take a yoga or other exercise class, it is possible that you can arrive before the other participants, or linger after they leave, in order to practice walking. Allow yourself time for some of the following preliminary exercises, and, at the beginning, about ten minutes for the actual walking. If this is a bodyspirit discipline that you find congenial, you may eventually want to extend that time.

A musical background to your walking can help you relax and focus, although some people prefer walking in silence. Recordings of plainsong or Gregorian chant evoke the walking of medieval monks in their cloisters yet do not compete with your own walking-rhythm because of their flowing nature. The latter is also true of a composition like Brian Eno's "Ambient Music for Airports," in which the notes merely hover in the air, rather than imposing a pattern that might interfere with your natural pace.

When you begin moving from foot to foot in a meditation walk, it is essential to be aware of where your weight is balanced on the ground. Begin by standing with the weight balanced equally over both feet. Picture yourself standing on a set of those old-fashioned scales held by a personification of Justice, with one foot on each side so that the scales are perfectly horizontal. You will be more stable if you bend your knees and "breathe" into your abdomen, because then your center of gravity is lower. Now move your weight entirely onto the left foot, so the left side of the imaginary scale goes down. Test your balance by lifting the right foot an inch or so. If you begin to lose your balance, just relax more into the left foot and keep breathing into the abdomen. Now shift your weight entirely to the right foot, lifting the left foot slightly once you have completed the weight change.

Now you are ready to take the first step forward. You may hold your arms in front of you as if you were carrying a bowl in your hands at waist level (some people find this helps them to balance) or let them fall at the sides. First, notice the alignment of the body, the contact of the feet with the ground, and the breath entering the abdomen. Now shift your weight entirely to the left foot, and once it is entirely on the left foot, lift your right foot to take a step forward. Your heel will touch the ground first. Then slowly place the foot on the floor, heel to toe, and shift your weight. Do not even *think* about taking the next step until all the weight is on the right foot.

Find the natural rhythm of your breathing as you walk, and be mindful of the rhythm; it helps you balance and focus. You may also wish to focus your mind by silently repeating a mantra (a word or short phrase) as you walk, such as "Come, my way, my truth, my life" or "Guide my feet in the way of peace." The Buddhist monk Thich Nhat Hanh writes that he teaches the young people in his community in France to repeat *"Oui, oui, oui"* as they inhale and *"Merci, merci, merci"* as they exhale.[6] "Yes" and "Thank you," in any language, would be excellent mantras to help us focus on the gift of God's presence with us every step of the way.

The key to this exercise is to have your full weight always on one foot or the other, never in between. The focus necessary for this relaxes the mind because it frees it from other thoughts, which is why it is called "meditation walking" or "walking meditation."

In walking meditation, our bodies themselves teach us the value of attentiveness to the present moment. When we slow down our walking, we may make some important connections. Letting our weight linger on the back foot when we should have our balance completely on the front one might remind us of what it feels like to cling to past resentments and regrets. On the other hand, if we think primarily of the *next* step rather than the one we are on, we will miss the satisfaction of being totally in balance on one foot. How often we do that with time itself, as we rush through our days without pausing to savor the goodness of the life God gave us. "Take time!" walking meditation tells us. Enjoy the rhythm of life intended for human nature, in which each moment is to be savored. "Now" is a holy word; it is in the present moment, no matter what its content of grief or joy, that God is found.

Walk, Look, and Listen

We live across the street from the beginning of a rough path through the Oberlin College arboretum, a wooded area that is deliberately left in its natural state. One of my favorite activities, except during peak mosquito season, is a more extroverted form of walking, quite different from the slow, deliberate walking described above. I move at whatever pace I like. I pause when I wish, standing on the bridge over the creek and watching it trickle or roar, as the case may be; bending down to examine a trout lily early in the spring; or looking skyward to try to spot the red-bellied woodpecker I hear calling from the highest branch of an oak. During these walks, I understand the presence of God in yet another way: as if I were reading a spiritual book written with the alphabet of the seasons and processes of the natural world. During these walks, I sometimes have to clamber over very old trees that have tumbled across the footpath and are slowly becoming part of the rich forest humus. I see green shoots striving for the sun, even through late winter snow. I hear the songs of birds and the chatter of squirrels going about their business, blissfully ignorant of the human events that can be so troubling. I see a design: God's design of interconnectedness, beauty, and, always, new life inning from death.

I am reminded of St. Teresa of Avila's comment that our senses are a doorway to prayer, because during these walks through the woods my senses are tuned to high volume. I truly hear and see. I smell the moist earth beneath my feet, the scent of wild honeysuckle, even the occasional whiff from the dairy farm a short way to the south. I feel my feet stumbling over a rock, or sinking in mud, or crackling over autumn leaves. I touch some moss, or a rough trunk of a tree. These walks convince me that in order to be fully alive I need to be in touch with the natural world. They make me understand the concept of "Gaia": simply another way of stating that the earth itself is a manifestation of the divine. *O God, how manifold are your works; in wisdom have you made them all!* (Psalm 104:25).

Friends of mine who are avid hikers take this kind of walking one step further, going to remote wilderness areas much more dramatic that our little arboretum across the road, and testing their own endurance at the same time. I have never had the opportunity for this kind of strenuous walking, but I have stood at the rim of the Grand Canyon and watched small figures following the winding path down to the Colorado River, and on the observation platform at the Jungfrau, shielding my eyes against the sun to squint at distant hikers making their way across a glacier.

You may not have an arboretum close at hand or be able to travel to wilderness areas, but all of us can get outdoors. When I am in Brooklyn, I like to walk down Smith Street. Traffic noises, airplanes overhead, voices speaking in various languages and accents, the laughter of children on the tree-shaded playground, the bells of the ubiquitous churches and the omnipresent ice-cream truck, all provide my senses with a doorway into the potential holiness of human life, just as the arboretum provides me with a window into the holiness of the natural world. And there is always the sky, from the gray ceiling on a rainy day to the sun slanting down the streets on a late winter afternoon.

Since many of us need to walk as part of our daily routine of work or school or shopping, this spiritual practice does not require us to set aside extra time. It merely requires us to remember a variation on the familiar caution: "Walk, Look, and Listen."

Pilgrimage

When the importance of arriving at a particular sacred destination is added to the practice of walking, the action becomes a pilgrimage. During the Middle Ages, thousands of pilgrims crossed Europe to visit the Holy Land, or, like Chaucer's Canterbury pilgrims, wended their way to more attainable shrines. Perhaps you remember walking somewhere in which it was the goal, as well as the journey, that was important.

When I was a twenty-one-year-old student at the Sorbonne in Paris, I was excited to learn about the annual student pilgrimage to Chartres Cathedral each May. I quickly signed up, rented a sleeping bag and backpack, which I filled with food that was much too heavy, and, on the appointed Saturday morning, reported at the train station to which the organizers had directed me. Disembarking at the first suburb outside Paris, we walked all day Saturday and slept that night in the barns dotting the wheat fields of that region. On Sunday morning we set forth again. I had never walked so far in my life, and my feet soon developed blisters. Whenever I thought I could not go another step, a song would begin that is still indelibly imprinted in my memory, *"Je vous salue, Marie, pleine de grâce,"* and the rhythm would carry me along, giving new life to my legs. But what really made the last miles of the pilgrimage possible was the sight of the spires of Chartres rising across the plains. The distance between the pilgrims streaming down the roads and the cathedral gradually narrowed, and we finally entered the town, trudged up the medieval streets, and, by late afternoon, gathered inside the great shadowy cathedral, mottled with stained-glass light. Our destination had indeed been worth the fatigue, even worth the blisters that took several days to heal.

Two of the abiding memories of that weekend are the effort of the journey and the incredible experience of completing it. Many centuries ago, King Alfred of Wessex described God as "the journey and the journey's end." Each step of my journey to Chartres was taken in the presence of the One who made the journey possible by giving me life in the first place. But the prayer and song we shared within that great cathedral were a sign of a destination beyond Chartres, beyond France, even beyond our planet: God, our eternal home.

Of course, one need not always walk on a pilgrimage; in modern times, planes, trains, and automobiles make the journeying easier. My most recent pilgrimage made use of the New York subway, when I made my way from Brooklyn to St. Paul's Chapel near the site of the World Trade Center. The effort was not so much physical as psychological. Would I be able to bear the sight of that void in the place where, in my days working at Trinity Church, Wall Street, I used to get off the "E" train, and where, one magical evening, my husband and I sat at a table, and watched the sun set behind the Statue of Liberty while having cocktails at Windows on the World? When I emerged from the Broadway-Nassau subway stop I was disoriented, not having realized that the twin towers had always been a landmark beckoning me in the right direction. But I found my way, entered St. Paul's with all its memories from 9/11, and then, with my heart in my mouth, walked one block farther west and stared into a void. I had come. I had made it. It was a place, for me, of the "intersection of the timeless with time," a destination symbolized by the cross made of two fallen beams from the World Trade Center, over which a fireman's coat had been draped, like the purple veils that cover the crosses of some churches during Lent.

There is a place of pilgrimage that carries happier memories. My maternal grandmother lived in East Smithfield, Pennsylvania, a hamlet just south of the New York border. My husband had heard many times about my childhood summers there, a world apart from my home in suburbia that, unlike my grandmother's house, had plumbing. Grandma Percy's nineteenth-century homestead sported pumps from which we drank ice cold water from the tin cup that hung nearby, an outhouse, a barn, and fragrant fields in which we children played by the hour. On a recent summer trip to New York, we decided to abandon our customary route and drive over the rolling hills to this place so full of childhood memories. After visiting the graves of my grandparents in the cemetery, we parked the car and walked into my past. My feet knew the way to the general store, now a hardware shop, to the site of the Baptist church where my grandfather had been the minister, and to the bandstand in the middle of the green. The house I remembered so well was recognizable, even without the outhouse and water pump. I pointed out to my husband exactly where they both had been. Although both house and town were modestly altered, the spirit of the little town was the same. Walking its sidewalks, some still tilting from the push of tree roots underneath (something that intrigued me no end when I was little), I was both child and adult at the same time. It was not just a visit; it was a pilgrimage. I had needed to put my body in that place once again, to experience it with eyes and ears and nose and footsteps.

The pilgrimages I describe have exactly that in common: getting the body somewhere. It may be through a long walk to a holy place. Or a trembling subway ride to the site of a historic calamity. Or an eager visit to a childhood mecca. Even in this electronic age, no videos will suffice to take us there. We have to be there ourselves, in the flesh.

Labyrinths

Walking a labyrinth involves following a specific pattern as you walk. It might be carved on the stone of a cathedral floor, as is the famous one at Chartres Cathedral in France, painted on a large canvas carpet, mowed into turf, or marked with ribbons or stones. The patterns all have one thing in common: they have no dead ends, as do mazes; instead, their winding path always leads to the center. Labyrinths have been known to the human race for over four thousand years, but the ones with which most westerners are familiar are found in European cathedrals. It is believed that they provided an opportunity for the faithful who were unable to make a pilgrimage to a sacred site like Jerusalem to make an alternative "pilgrimage" by walking the labyrinth within the safety of a cathedral instead.

Besides hearkening back to this history, it is interesting to remember our own childhood fascination with stepping in patterns. Hopscotch, which challenged my ability to hop and balance within the squares chalked on the asphalt street adjoining our front lawn, is still played by children today. Sometimes, when my parents would take me to our downtown shopping area, I, like generations before me, would make a game of avoiding the cracks in the sidewalk: "Step on a crack, break your mother's back!" Watch children on a patterned tile floor. Perhaps they notice it better than we do because they are closer to it, for they find it endlessly fascinating. I first encountered a cathedral labyrinth, in fact, in the company of a seven-year-old, who, as the rest of our group toured Ely Cathedral, took my hand and raced through the labyrinth on the floor of the nave with me.

I walked more slowly one summer afternoon through the turf labyrinth on the windswept summit of St. Catherine's Hill overlooking the city of Winchester, England. It was haunting to trace the footsteps of the long-ago generations who created this pattern high above the cathedral. It seemed I would never reach the center. Then, shortly after the path had taken me back almost to the circumference, I found myself suddenly at the center. Indoor labyrinths draw me to more introspection, but the outdoor one, accompanied by birdsong, the fragrance of sweet grass, and the sound of distant traffic, was exhilarating.

Walking a labyrinth can be done at any pace: a slow meditation walk, your natural stride, even skipping or dancing. We bring to the experience who we are and what we need at the time.

Some suggestions follow about a variety of ways in which you might use this spiritual and physical tool for prayer. Before you begin, pause for a moment and place this experience in God's hands. When you finally reach the center, pause again for as long as you wish before retracing your steps.

Enter the labyrinth with no expectations or plans about what will happen. As in a walking meditation, just walk, keeping your mind quiet and receptive.

Make the labyrinth walk an exercise in noticing the breath. Coordinate your breathing with your stride, allowing your body to find its own natural rhythm.

Reflect on your life now and listen to what the labyrinth can teach you as you walk. One woman tells the story of facing an overwhelming pile of tax forms that she needed to complete. Her financial advisor told her, "Don't worry, there is a linear path through it." She says that she laughed as she realized that the tax forms were not a maze but a labyrinth: "All we have to do is put one foot in front of the other. We'll answer question 1, then question 2. I can cope with that."[7]

You can walk holding a particular prayer in your mind. Perhaps there is someone you know who needs your intercessions. Or perhaps you seek guidance in dealing with some problem or decision. You can even hold your hands, palms up, before you as you walk, offering these intentions to God.

You can use a mantra or a repetitive chant as you walk, to focus and quiet the mind.

You can walk the way of the mystics: Purgative, Illuminative, and Unitive. *Purgative:* as you enter the labyrinth, let the things that block your relationship with God fall away, step by step by step. *Illuminative:* in the center, pause, opening your mind to insights that might well up within you. *Unitive:* as you exit, you will be taking what you have learned at the center into the world, doing the work God has guided you to do.

You can create your own way of using the labyrinth. Take the hand of a seven-year-old. Or read your Bible as you walk. Be open to the Spirit, and see what happens!

I once arrived at a cathedral ready to include a labyrinth walk as part of a spiritual exercises workshop, only to find that the canvas labyrinth they owned had been lent to a parish church and had not been returned. Instead, I suggested that participants go to a space in the cathedral where they could walk their own imaginary pattern, a labyrinth of their own making. It worked wonderfully, and can be done by any of us, any time. With our bodies we can trace the journey of prayer: to the center of ourselves, where we can be most in touch with God. We can remain there, dwelling in that place that is so small and yet so immense, breathing in God's love and healing power. Then we can make the journey outward, along a path of our own devising. The labyrinths that are carved, mowed, or painted are only there as tools to help us make that ultimate journey, which we can make anywhere and at any time.

*

HATHA YOGA

Among the many philosophies that originated in ancient India, none is better known now than yoga. The founder of the discipline, Patañjali, has been identified through his writings in the *Yoga Sutras,* believed to have been written during the third century B.C.E.

The word *sutra* means a "thread." In his book, Patañjali describes the threads that, when woven together, can create a life in which we are unified in body and spirit. The first two threads are the *yamas,* or ethical principles, and the *niyamas,* codes that help us live according to those principles. The next two are the *asanas,* physical postures that have been described as "dynamic internal dances," and *pranayama,* the breathing practice that accompanies the *asanas.* The final four threads are *pratyahara,* bringing the senses under control; *dharana,* the stilling of the mind; *dhyana,* meditation; and *samadhi,* the union of the self and the divine.

The word "yoga" comes from the Sanskrit word *yug,* which means to yoke, or join together. The various types of yoga—yogas of devotion *(bhatkti yoga),* knowledge *(jnana yoga),* action *(karma yoga),* and inner concentration *(raja yoga)*—are designed to help us join together the self and the divine. Hatha yoga is a branch of raja yoga and includes postures, breathing techniques, and meditation. *Hatha* is really two separate words, *ha* and *tha,* which mean literally "sun" and "moon," suggesting the joining of two entities, such as dark and light, body and spirit, or even the right and left hemispheres of the brain.

Some of you may already be familiar with my book *An Invitation to Christian Yoga.*[8] It tells the story of my discovering an incredible sense of centering and calm during a yoga class taught in a high school gym many years ago. I remembered that class and what it had done for me when I entered a theological seminary and began a special ministry in teaching about spirituality and prayer. I taught one of my first Christian yoga classes at the seminary, and then offered them weekly at Trinity Church, Wall Street, where I worked after graduation. Most of my students there came from offices in the financial district to seek some breathing space in the middle of their frenetic day. It was an easy matter to "Christianize" this ancient practice; after all, our bodies have the same skeletal design and musculature no matter what our brand of faith.

On occasion, I have been approached by people who are hesitant about the use of yoga, concerned that the practice will draw them away from their Christian faith. I have assured my inquirers that the human body does not vary from religion to religion, and that the exercises of yoga are often exactly the same movements used by dancers and students in physical fitness classes. Yoga exercises are religion-neutral; we bring to them our own belief. What is Christian yoga? The short answer is: Christian yoga is yoga done by a Christian.

Even the Sanskrit concepts at the beginning of this section sound strangely familiar when translated into English and interpreted within the context of our own culture. When I have attended a hatha yoga class taught within a Hindu philosophical framework, we have chanted "Om" or "Aum," the word for deity in Sanskrit. In the Hindu Scripture, the *Bhagavad-Gîtâ,* the deity says, "I am the father of the world, the mother, the supporter, the grandsire. I am the object of knowledge, the purifier. I am the syllable *Aum."* This verse evokes for me God's voice from the burning bush in the story of Moses: "I am who I am." It also reminds me of the struggles among Christians in the early centuries of the church's history to articulate the ways they had come to know God. These struggles finally produced the doctrine of the Trinity, for which language is still inadequate. I enjoy seeing the parallels between *Bhagavad-Gîtâ*'s description of the deity as "Father/mother/supporter/grandsire, object of knowledge/purifier" and some of the words we use today: Father/Mother/ Creator,

Son/Jesus/Incarnate One, Holy Spirit/Holy Wisdom/Healer. God, despite our labels, remains a mystery we cannot capture through ordinary speech.

Hatha yoga is an ancient yet also contemporary way of "tuning the body." However, it is different from most western exercise because it is noncompetitive. We neither compete with other people nor with our own expectations of ourselves, but accept, while also trying to extend, the capabilities of our own bodies. Ideally, we do not merely copy the instructor, but allow the movement to come from within us, initiated by the energy and the rhythm of our breath.

Christian yoga is sometimes accompanied by the repetition of Christian prayers or verses of Scripture. A sequence known as the "Salute to the Sun," for example, can be accompanied by the petitions of the Lord's Prayer, so appropriate to the movements that it is uncanny. A class typically includes instruction in yoga postures and stretches, attention to breathing and relaxation, plus a period of meditation.

Here is an example of what you can expect from a yoga class.

Begin by standing erect and inhaling, as you reach toward the ceiling. As you exhale, bring the arms out to the sides, so your body is in a cruciform posture. Finally, bring your hands to the center of the chest as you inhale, and out in front of you as you exhale. You will read later, in the chapter on "Praying Through the Body," that this is a "movement mantra," a salute to the God who created us, redeems us, and is the Spirit within and among us. Repeat this movement two more times. This movement prayer creates the context in which we will do hatha yoga.

This next exercise demonstrates the way that yoga can relax and stretch our muscles. If it is difficult for you to do on the floor, you can try it seated on the edge of a chair with one leg extended straight in front of you.

Sit on the floor with both legs stretched out directly in front of you and the spine straight, as if your head were growing toward the sky. Bend the left leg and place the sole of the left foot against the inside of the right leg, somewhere between the knee and the groin, letting the left knee drop outward. Try to keep both "sit-bones" (the bottoms of the hip bones) squarely on the floor.

Inhale as you lift both arms in front of you and up above your head, looking upward. Then exhale and bend forward toward the extended leg, folding like a book being closed. Reach with the arms and the chest, contracting the abdominal muscles and bending at the hips. Breathe normally and rest in that position, letting your body relax toward the leg without any strain. Feel the heaviness of your head and your shoulders and imagine a hinge releasing at the base of your spine. As you remain there, mentally send your breath into that hinge. Do not *try* to stretch; just let it happen naturally, because of the weight of your upper body and the relaxation of your muscles.

Return to your original position by inhaling, as you exhale and contract the abdominal muscles, while reaching with your arms out and then upward.

Now repeat the exercise with the other leg, placing the right foot against the inside of the left leg.

Have you discovered one of the secrets of yoga: *try less, do more?* Physiologists tell us that sometimes our effort to stretch can be counterproductive. When we try too hard to lengthen our muscles, they react by shortening, tightening themselves in order to protect themselves from injury. It is the act of relaxing into one position, remaining there, and breathing that lengthens our muscles.

This exercise teaches me much about respecting reality. I have to accept my limitations, not comparing myself to the young sylph who might be next to me in yoga class. (I should not be looking at her, anyway, because yoga is best done with closed eyes.) By relaxing into what I *can* do, rather than fighting to accomplish what I *cannot* do, I become more flexible. It is my body's way of teaching me not merely about physical flexibility, but about other ways of stretching.

After I do this exercise, I feel younger and healthier. It reminds me that stretching is absolutely necessary as we grow older. Unless we extend our muscles, they will shorten, slowly but surely.

The same is true with the rest of life. It is tempting not to make the effort to stretch ourselves, but to settle into what seems comfortable and unthreatening: our familiar social set, our own neighborhood, our habitual ways of thinking, our usual activities. Just as my body wakes up when I stretch it, so my mind and my heart awaken when I remember to stretch them. Meeting new people, especially someone who is a different age or a different nationality; learning new things by delving into a subject I know nothing about; traveling to new places; trying new activities—all of these stretch the rest of me.

When I perform this particular exercise, I am not only stretching; I am bending. It is reminiscent of a verse from Psalm 5, "I will bow down before your holy temple in awe of you" (Ps. 5:7). Using a prayer like this at the beginning of an exercise is also a way to perform yoga exercises as a Christian: the movements can suggest words, as well as serving as a metaphor for some of life's wisdom. Above all, they can become, in themselves, a prayer of mindfulness, as we focus on ourselves as bodyspirit—wondrous, fully alive creations of God.

Sit on the edge of a straight chair with the feet flat on the floor for the second exercise, the spinal twist. Begin with your hands on your lap. To stay lifted in this pose, rise up through the top of the head as if a tuft of hair in the middle of your scalp were being pulled by a string, and imagine that your sit-bones are glued to the seat of the chair.

Inhale. Then exhale, imagine you are dropping your shoulder blades into two pockets on your back directly below them. Picture your spine as a spiral staircase, and, as you do, begin to turn slowly to your left, beginning the twist at the tailbone. As you twist, there will then be a lift at each "step" of the staircase. Think of the ribs, rather than the spine, doing the work. Feel the left ribs opening out from the sternum, or breastbone, and closing into the spine, while the right ribs do the partner work of opening out from the spine and wrapping around into the right side of the sternum. Allow a sense of lift and relaxation to make room for the inner organs, like the kidneys, which are floating within the space of your body. Let your spine remain soft, like an infant's. Allow your arms to follow the twist naturally, with the left arm moving behind you and the right arm curving across the front of the body toward the left, with both hands at approximately waist level.

As you move into the twist, make sure that you stop if there is any discomfort. As in all yoga movements, you can protect yourself from injury by close attentiveness to the way the body is feeling. Hold the twist briefly, then return to your original position.

Repeat the exercise, twisting to the right side; then repeat on each side once more.

This exercise is not only essential for those of us who want to back our cars safely out of our driveways, but helps to maintain a youthful freedom of movement in all of our daily activities. It also reminds us of the need to keep "looking around" at a broader perspective, rather than merely becoming fixated on one point of view. You can perform this movement either with the eyes closed, focusing on the way the spine, the ribs, and the organs feel, or with eyes open, so that it becomes a "seeing meditation" as you gaze at each object that comes into view as you turn.

A typical yoga class includes attention to breathing, as we have already noted in the section on "Breathing." Toward the end of the class the students rest on the floor on their backs, while the teacher helps them release any remaining tension by inviting them to relax the muscles in various parts of the body, beginning with the feet, while they are named. To experience what a class is like, you may wish to include both slow diaphragmatic breathing and progressive relaxation now, gently scanning your body from toe to head for tension and then releasing it.

It was at this point that my first teacher would suggest that we spend some time imagining a lotus or a candle, helping our minds also to relax. This would last about five minutes, and then the most difficult part of my first yoga classes in the high school gym took place. The teacher said, "Now move and stretch, turn over on your side, and get up." Instead, I found myself wanting to linger, because the tuning and relaxation of my body and mind had initiated an openness of spirit that had readied me for prayer. That is why I always follow yoga exercises with time simply to be silent in God's presence.

Henri Nouwen writes that "to pray means to open your hands before God. It means slowly relaxing the tension which squeezes your hands together and accepting your existence with an increasing readiness, not as a possession to defend, but as a gift to receive."[9] Hatha yoga can enable us not only to unclench our tight fists in order to accept the blessing of life, but also to release the tension of our whole bodies. This ancient Hindu discipline helps me to hold fast to the God I know through Jesus Christ, "from whom the whole body, nourished and held together by its ligaments and sinews, grows with a growth that is from God" (Colossians 2:19).

✳

TAI CHI

It was in the 1960s that the world began to see pictures of groups of Chinese doing tai chi chuan on the streets at dawn. Even today, a quarter of a billion people—more than the total population of the United States—practice tai chi daily in China. We also can observe and learn tai chi in our own country: in universities, YMCAs and YWCAs, health clubs, nursing homes, and parks. Observers inevitably describe the discipline as a "ballet," for its gentle flowing movements are beautiful to watch. And, indeed, when we ourselves learn to perform them, it feels like a dance.

The history of tai chi, or tai chi chuan, is told in two versions. The one I enjoy most is a legend set in a mountainous region in China, about eight hundred years ago. The "Taoist immortal," Chang San-feng, is asleep and begins to dream. "A heavenly presence demonstrates to him the fundamental movements of Tai Chi Chuan." Awakening, Chang remembers what he has been shown and realizes that he must share this with the world. As he sets forth and passes through a village, he learns that one hundred brigands are plaguing the inhabitants. "When the brigands come again, Chang resorts to his Tai Chi movements, mobilizes an art of gentleness into an art of devastation, and like one of the raging dragons which live on the peaks of Wu-tang, he scatters them like autumn leaves."[10]

The more pedestrian explanation of tai chi's origin tells us that it evolved from previously existing styles of boxing. In the late eighteenth century, the martial artist Wang Tsung-yueh formalized its movements. As in the legend, it was an encounter with an adversary that gave tai chi wider circulation. One day, Wang made a disapproving remark about some martial arts training he had witnessed in a village belonging to the Chen family and was challenged to back up his words. He defeated the family members in single combat, thereby making such an impression that the village leaders asked him to stay and teach them. The Chen family continued to develop what Wang had taught them, often incorporating their favorite movements from other martial arts.

This practice of making the tai chi form "your own" resulted eventually in several styles, each one usually bearing the family name of the founder, such as Chen, Yang, Old Wu, New Wu, Sun, and Hao. That is why, should you learn the tai chi form from one teacher and then study with another, you may encounter a quite different set of movements. My own teacher had learned the Yang style from an elderly Chinese woman in San Francisco. My teacher was a former ballet dancer and I suspect that his style owed something to that background, for tai chi is somewhat like the oral folk tale tradition, in which stories change subtly as they are passed down from person to person.

Tai chi became associated with the religious tradition of Taoism when Wang Tsung-yueh formalized the movements. Taoism, a Chinese philosophy dating from about 300 B.C.E., grew out of keen observation of the natural world. It is often traced back to a legendary figure named Lao Tzu, the traditional author of the great classic *Tao Te Ching*. Taoism speaks of the polarity within each of us of *yin* and *yang*, another way of describing the human potential for both creation and destruction. Its symbol is a circle, divided by a double curve into two parts: one part is black with a white circle in it; the other part is white with a black circle within.

A tai chi teacher would advise the student to perform the movements of tai chi with circularity, fluidity, and coordination, in order to direct the flow of *chi* (life-energy) throughout the body. This concept may seem strange to westerners. However, I must confess that, rather than finding this language about *chi* alien when I first heard the term, I recognized my own experience of the body's energy. I understand it as yet another way of describing the process of our breath carrying oxygen and renewal to the cells.

Tai chi is usually done slowly, with the mind thoroughly concentrated on the movement. It is believed to promote health by improving the flow of *chi* from the lower psychic center (a place three inches below the navel called the *tan tien*) throughout the entire body. (It is worth remembering this when you read the section about Pilates.) As in hatha yoga, you breathe primarily through the diaphragm, helping you achieve a lower center of gravity. Its movements benefit not only the body: the practice calms the mind and thus enhances mental health as well.

Since describing even an abbreviated tai chi "form" or sequence of movements would take an entire book, I hope that the following exercises will at least enable you to experience how it feels to practice this ancient way of integrating bodyspirit. Move slowly, as if you were doing the exercises under water. Picture the atmosphere around you as "thicker than air" as you move through it.

The first exercises in the "Walking" section, which help you to discover your feet and to shift your weight, are a good preparation for tai chi. Tai chi, like walking, is dependent on a mindful shifting of your weight as you move from foot to foot.

One of the so-called temple exercises, which Asian monks and nuns use morning and night, is called the "Prayer Wheel." It is easiest to learn this by learning the movement of the arms and the feet separately.

> *The feet:* Begin by standing on both feet. Then lift up your right foot and step forward, placing first your heel and then the rest of the foot on the ground, shifting the weight. The other foot remains on the floor but your weight is not on it. Now shift the weight back onto the left foot. Continue shifting the weight back and forth, trying to keep the body erect and your head on the same level throughout.

> Keep practicing this movement until it becomes easy and natural.

The arms: Begin with your elbows bent, close to the body near the hips, and the palms of the hands facing one another approximately at shoulder height. Then bring your hands, with the palms still straight and facing one another, down along your sides. Once your arms are straight, circle them in front of you and back up to the original position, as if your palms were attached to the rims of two big wagon-wheels attached to your sides.

Practice this movement, also, until it comes naturally.

Combine feet and arms: It should not be too difficult now to combine the movements of the arms and the feet. You begin with the hands up near the shoulders and then circle them downward and out in a circular motion as you step forward. They reach the bottom of the circle when you are on your forward foot, then continue the circle as you shift your weight to the back foot, until they arrive at the starting point. I find that it helps to exhale as I step forward and to inhale as I shift to the back foot. The whole body does indeed become a "wheel"—actually two wheels!

When this comes easily with the right foot stepping forward, shift legs and lead with the left foot. Repeat the "Prayer Wheel" anywhere from ten to thirty times on each side.

Perhaps you have seen prayer wheels, which actually come from the Tibetan Buddhist tradition, demonstrating the eclectic history of tai chi. They consist of a cylinder inside of which are pieces of paper inscribed with sacred phrases. As the cylinder is spun or twirled, it revolves around a central pole. The turning of the wheel represents the constant impetus of the devotee's prayers circling toward God. In this exercise, we ourselves are the prayer wheel. As we trace a circle with our hands, we are sending the concerns of our heart toward God.

The first movements of the tai chi form taught to me demonstrate the "feel" of *chi* energy in a way that always surprises participants in my workshops.

Stand with both feet solidly on the floor and the knees relaxed and arms hanging at your sides. Then, as if the air underneath your arms were surging upward, like a sudden rush of air from a sidewalk grating, inhale and, keeping the arms hanging straight, allow the "air" to raise the palms slowly, bending at the wrist so that the hands are horizontal or parallel to the ground. Exhale and let them drop down again.

Again, inhale, and now raise the arms, keeping both hands and arms relaxed and rounded, as if the surge of air were billowing up beneath them.

Inhale and let them drop down, not to the sides this time, but in front of you, and make a circle with the left hand on top and the right below, as if you were holding a small exercise ball about six to eight inches in diameter. Hold that ball shape in front of you, then slowly move your weight to the right foot as you inhale, taking the "ball" with you, in a long, relaxed motion. Exhale and turn over the "ball," so that the right hand is on top and left hand is below, and shift the weight to the left foot.

At this point, take note of how your body feels. Still holding the "ball" in your hands, imagine that it can expand and contract. Experiment with it, bringing your hands closer together and then farther away from each other. What do you feel?

If you are doing this in the company of other people, turn to someone and discover what happens when the flat but relaxed palms of your right hands, held at chest or shoulder level, approach each other slowly. (You have "dropped" the imaginary ball by now.) It is quite evident that there is energy emanating from your palm and your neighbor's.

In the west, the use of therapeutic touch among nurses relies on this field of energy: as the nurse's healing hand, held only slightly above the skin, scans the patient's body, it can pick up areas of dis-ease and give forth its own healing energy, adding the energy of another human being to more conventional methods of healing. When I pause at the altar rail to lay hands on someone who remains there for healing prayers after receiving communion, I try to remember the healing energy of my own body as a channel of God's power—the ultimate *chi*.

This exercise weaves together the wisdom of several traditions: Taoist, Native American, and Christian. It uses movements from tai chi, salutes the four directions of the compass, and reveals wisdom about what it means to live as a Christian. Through it we express the stability and freedom we find when we are in touch with the Ground of our Being, whose Spirit is the source of effective action in the world.

Begin by standing firmly on the floor, facing east, with knees relaxed and slightly bent, and your hands at your side. As you inhale, bend your elbows, cup your hands, and bring your hands up to the center of your body at about chest level, picturing yourself gathering energy up from the earth. Exhale and take a step forward onto your right foot, flatten your palms outward, and picture yourself pushing that energy straight out in front of you. Stretch your arms only as far as you can do so without needing to tilt your body. When your arms are fully stretched, just release your hands at the wrists, allowing the hands to relax and drop.

This last movement always reminds me of the need to recognize my limits. I can remember times when I was so eager to accomplish something that I kept pushing when it was no longer effective to do so. Many of the movements in tai chi have this element of "letting go," reminding us to stay within our physical and spiritual limits. They bring to mind the Mbuti, the African tribe that believes we each are surround-ed by an invisible sphere that provides our identity and a sense of security. Should the body move so quickly that it leaves the space before our identity has had time to catch up, the individual becomes disoriented. The Mbuti people call this *wazi wazi,* a famil-iar enough experience for most of us in this fast-paced world.[11]

Now inhale and rock back onto your left foot, turning your hands palms up in a receptive position, as you twist your upper body to the left, moving your arms and hands along a quarter-circle at approximately shoulder height to your left, so that you are looking north.

Finally, exhale and transfer your weight to the right foot, beginning by swivel-ing on the right heel as you turn the whole body to the south and bring the left foot alongside the right in order to rest. As you do this, bring both hands back down to the sides, in the neutral beginning posture.

If you repeat this exercise three more times, you will have saluted the four directions of the compass, a way of affirming that all parts of the globe—the continents and seas, forests and fields, canyons and cities—are holy.

Think, too, about the four elements as you move through this exercise. First, as we draw the energy up from below, we join with the *earth* in praising our Creator. As we push our arms forward with our exhalation, we send the *fire* of love out into the world. As we turn gently to the left with receptive palms cupped upward, we give thanks for the life-giving qualities of *water.* As we turn to our right, and settle in a new direction, we show our willingness to be blown by the *air* of God's Spirit.

When you have become adept at moving in a clockwise direction, balance yourself by moving in a counterclockwise direction, stepping forward with the left rather than the right foot at the beginning, and continuing the movements as a mirror image of the ones above.

When I lead conferences for clergy, I suggest that the practice of tai chi can teach them about the use of their bodies in liturgy. They take some time to truly connect with the ground beneath them when they stand, knowing where their weight is sinking into the floor. Then they perform certain liturgical actions as if the movements were a form of tai chi, breathing with the diaphragm so as to feel centered. They make the sign of the cross in blessing as if moving underwater, and raise an imaginary chalice as if the atmosphere around them is thicker than air. The increase in their body's "presence" when they move like that is extraordinary.

It is a fascinating exercise to take some ordinary or habitual activity and perform it in slow motion in order to become more aware of what muscles we use and where our body weight is balanced. One of my piano teachers taught me to practice in a slow and very focused way from time to time when I was learning a piece, and it worked wonders. You might try the same thing with sweeping the floor, washing the car, or swinging a golf club, just as an experiment.

Whether we do a tai chi form or our own versions thereof, tai chi teaches us balance, as we put one foot in front of the other to go about our daily activities. It helps us balance our spirits as well, as we learn to become clear channels of the energy that is the *chi* of God coursing through every part of our body and our lives.

PILATES

Joseph Pilates, the inventor of the Pilates method of body-conditioning, was born in Germany in 1880. Because he was a frail child, he later became passionate about physical fitness and developed a regimen performed on an exercise mat that combined eastern and western principles in order to strengthen the body and focus the mind. News of his system spread throughout Germany, and the Kaiser summoned Pilates to train his elite troops. Since Pilates was an ardent pacifist, he fled to England, where he was interned in a prison camp for the duration of World War I. There, he continued to work on his system, teaching it to his fellow prisoners and to the guards. Eventually, as trainer to the boxer Max Schmelling, he opened a Pilates studio in New York City, where his method was discovered by dancers such as Martha Graham, Ruth St. Denis, Ted Shawn, and George Balanchine.

The Pilates technique centers on the concept of the "core": the deep abdominal muscles that form the body's "powerhouse" by creating a stable, strong base. The energy for the exercises is initiated in this area; it is the source of all movement, even of the hands and the feet. This emphasis on our center helps the muscles of the right and left sides of the body begin to balance one another, since most of us are slightly lopsided. The quality of the movement is controlled and fluid, as if you were moving through something thick, like molasses. The number of times an exercise is performed is not important; it is better to do a movement four times with the proper attention and technique than to do it many times without focusing on it. As one Pilates instructor writes, "When you work your body without engaging the mind, you are performing only half a workout."[12]

The first step in learning Pilates technique is discovering the abdominal core, or "powerhouse." The following exercises will help you locate this center deep within your pelvis, so necessary to doing every Pilates movement correctly and safely.

Lie on your back, with your knees bent and your feet on the floor. Imagine that there are shoelaces from your pubic bone up to your navel and that you are pulling the laces, beginning at the bottom, as if you were lacing up hiking boots or ice skates. Do not move the position of your pelvis; just let the inner muscles do the work. Do you feel your deep abdominal muscles drawing inward and upward?

Lift your head in this position. Do these muscles become even firmer?

Lie on your back, with your knees bent and your feet flat on the floor. Visualize a clockface imprinted on your abdomen. Twelve o'clock is at your pubic bone, three o'clock is at your right hip, six o'clock is at your navel, and nine o'clock is at your left hip. The clockface should remain perfectly flat in the following exercise. It sounds easy, but the effort it entails draws into play the deep core muscles of the abdomen.

Lift your right foot an inch or so off the ground. You will be tempted to compensate by letting your left hip roll outward, but do not let it happen. Replace the foot on the floor and repeat with the left foot, remembering to keep the imaginary clockface completely still.

When you have achieved this, take it to another level of difficulty. Raise your right leg vertically, keeping your abdomen absolutely level, and make small circles with the entire leg in one direction, then in the other. You can feel the ripple of the deep muscles of the core, as your abdomen attempts to remain stable.

Now repeat with the other leg. Do not be surprised if stability on one side is easier to achieve than on the other. That is true for virtually everyone, and is proof of Joseph Pilate's thesis that we all need to renew the balance within our bodies.

This next movement is best done initially with a theraband: a long piece of elastic used for exercise. (These can be easily obtained at a sporting goods store, or ordered online—simply google "theraband." They come in various degrees of stretchiness, and a medium to strong theraband is recommended for this exercise.)

Sit up straight with your legs extended in front of you and the theraband looped around your feet. Holding an end of the theraband in each hand, pull your abdominal muscles in and up, initiating a curve in your lower spine so that your torso assumes the shape of the letter "c."

Very slowly roll down your spine, vertebra by vertebra, thinking of pushing your feet away from your abdomen to stretch the theraband away from you as you roll down until your head touches the floor. Then bring your head forward and use your "powerhouse" (abdominal muscles) to roll up again to a sitting position. Alternatively, roll just a part of the way down and then up again; the important part is finding the strength in those core muscles, rather than rolling down all the way.

When you have discovered the deep core muscles while lying down, stand up. Draw in those muscles again, as if you were lacing up the same imaginary shoelaces. Does it feel as if your back is better supported now? Do you feel more stable? Try walking in this way. Does walking feel different as well? Take a few minutes to go through some everyday motions, like taking a grocery bag out of a shopping cart, or running the vacuum cleaner, or getting into and out of the car, to note how much more stable and strong you feel.

The first winter after I had discovered Pilates, the snow that fell on Christmas Eve remained for several weeks. I often took down the cross-country skis from the rack beside our garage door and glided down our driveway and across the street to the golf course on the other side. I had suspected I was discovering new stability through discovering my core abdominal muscles, but skiing during these weeks provided dramatic proof. I have a long and flexible back, which courts disaster even on the gentle hills of the course. Often the top of my torso wobbles, disconnected from my pelvis, and more than once I have landed in a heap. That particular winter, I discovered the trick of "lacing up" before I started down a hill, and never once did I fall. I was also very aware of the difference in my stability when a distraction—a scampering squirrel causing me to turn my head, or wandering thoughts luring me away from what I was doing—caused my balance to become precarious once again.

The spiritual concept most akin to the physical idea of the core, or "powerhouse," in Pilates is the word "centering." In recent times, "centering prayer" has been used to describe wordless waiting upon God, just being still in God's presence, like Quakers sitting silently in their meetings centering their attention on the inner light of the divine presence. It is a way of prayer to which I myself am particularly drawn, and I have discovered that it has the same effect on daily life as Pilates awareness has on skiing. When I have spent twenty minutes to half an hour early in the day finding my center in God, I move through the following hours with a stability that is missing when I have neglected that regular practice.

I think of St. Patrick, who, according to his hymn "St. Patrick's Breastplate," protected himself from danger not by an outward physical shield but by binding to himself "the strong name of the Trinity." Pilates reminds me that the "whole armor of God" is deeply interior, not something merely on the surface. I put it on by being with God, and through that time of being with God, I am given a measure of God's strength, God's stability.

Pilates is not a "quick fix" type of exercise. It is a slow process of finding and then working from our center, with both our body and our mind. Once discovered, we must keep it up, or those deep muscles will forget their strength.

The same is true of my prayer. It would be great to discover stability in God through a religious "high" of some kind, but it doesn't happen often, nor does it usually last when it does. Instead, we are called just to show up: to be there, in that unseen place that is our "center," with our body, our mind, our heart, and our strength.

*

ALEXANDER TECHNIQUE

Frederick Matthias Alexander was born in 1869 on Tasmania, an island off the coast of Australia. Unable to pursue higher education because of poverty, he took a job with a local tin mining company, although the stage had been his love since childhood. In his spare time, he learned the recitations—narratives and poetry from literature—so popular in his day, and eventually decided to throw all his energy into developing a career in the theater.

Unfortunately, Alexander's voice often gave him problems. Doctors could only suggest successively longer periods of vocal rest in order to cure him, but this did not work. Finally, one night, he lost his voice completely and left the stage in despair. That was a turning point for him: he decided to find out for himself what was wrong. He devoted himself to observation, surrounding himself with mirrors as an aid, and finally discovered that every effort to speak was accompanied by a tendency to pull his head backward and down, caused by a small but perceptible contraction of the muscles at the back of his neck. At the same time, he lifted his chest and hollowed his back. He did this not only when he was reciting on stage, but in the ordinary actions of daily life.

Alexander decided to substitute for these habits the conscious movement of the head and body upward. His vocal health returned and he resumed his theatrical career. After much persuasion to share his secrets, he soon took on another profession: a teacher of the Alexander Technique. He taught his pupils to understand the use of their bodies as a whole, allowing freedom of muscular function and balance on the skeletal frame. The internal organs could then have room to function well, the circulatory system could operate freely, and the spinal cord was relieved of uneven pressure. It was a unique approach to posture not as a static pose, but as a dynamic way to use the body efficiently.

The first principal of the Alexander Technique is the basic orientation of the head and torso upward. This language must be understood, however, not as our forcing or manipulating our bodies, but as thinking about them in a different way. Alexander instructors are fond of saying "let the head move forward and up it's just a thought!" To actually *pull* the head up is to violate the Alexander principle of not forcing the body.

To discover the effects of this way of thinking about the head and its movement upward, first do the following movements as you ordinarily do them.

Seated in a chair, turn your head slowly to look to the left, then to the right. Tip your head back to look up at the ceiling, then look down at the floor.

What do you notice? Do you feel any tension or tightness in your neck? Do any of these movements affect your breathing?

Now, do the same movements but begin with what Alexander called the Basic Movement. Picture your head being gently pulled up by a string attached to the top of the skull, as if you were a marionette. If you think of your ears reaching for the ceiling as well, your head will be in the correct position. You do not need to exert yourself to hold your head up if it is balanced properly on the sturdy base of the top vertebra of your spine.

Before you turn your head to each side, notice the balance of your head on your spine and then allow it to reach upward, as if you were growing taller. Before you look upward or downward, do the same thing. Was turning your head, and then looking upward and downward, easier this time?

Now stand, and repeat this Basic Movement. Does this "upward thinking" help the rest of your body fall into place, and give you greater freedom of movement? Your body is a like a flexible column, and when energy and movement are directed up through the top of that column, with the whole torso following the upward movement of the head, the body will work more efficiently.

Alexander suggested that every single movement should begin with thinking about the movement of the head forward and up from the body. In walking, the upward thinking will move you forward. In getting up from a chair, the most efficient movement begins with leaning forward and standing by "leading with the head," letting the body follow the direction in which the head is moving.

Alexander, who so closely observed the way he used—and misused—his body, reminds me of the way that bad habits can accumulate over the years and create problems, especially as we age. When I was a teenager, it was fashionable to carry our heavy schoolbooks, carefully stacked on top of our loose-leaf notebooks, on one hip. Because I am right-handed I chose the right hip, and for six years I walked lopsided to the bus stop and down the middle school and high school corridors. When I began having pain in my right hip a few years ago, my teacher Deborah took one look. "Why, your right leg is longer than the left!" An inefficient physical habit (and definitely an inefficient way of carrying books in all weathers!) had done its work during my growing years, just as Alexander's pulling his head backward and down had paralyzed his vocal cords.

It is good stewardship of our bodies to evaluate our physical habits in order to discern whether we could be harming our bodies because of the way we sit or get out of chairs, or carry books, for that matter. Just as destructive emotional or psychological habits can upset the balance of our lives and sour our relationships, so too the body's bad habits take their toll over a lifetime. The goal of Alexander's method, and of others like Feldenkrais, Laban, or Bartenieff, is the practical one of helping us become aware of the ways we move so that we can live more efficiently. For that, we often need someone else to point out the harmful patterns of which we are not aware, just as a good friend might confront us about attitudes or behaviors that are destructive.

Alexander also reminds me of the power of our thought processes. In my "Body Reeducation and Alignment" course, our teacher would have us lie on the floor, merely picturing changes in our body. For example, we were to visualize the back of the pelvis widening and the spine lengthening downward. We were amazed when we stood up and began walking, for we had new freedom of movement in the hip joints: changes had happened without specific physical exercises to accomplish them. It makes perfect sense, however. The brain sent the messages to the neurological system while we rested, and when we stood up and moved, the messages made the rest of the journey. It is no more amazing than my sending a friend an e-mail that hovers in cyberspace until my friend activates her computer so that it becomes visible on the screen.

In this world so full of mystery, it seems to make sense that our thought and our prayers hover in a kind of spiritual cyberspace, as well. How we think certainly affects our actions. I wonder if our thoughts also influence the world, for good or for ill. When I have been in the presence of the violent energy of a person who is extremely angry, I know that I feel it, whether the person lashes out at me physically or not. Afterward, when I enter a home full of love and peace, I take a grateful breath and settle in to the atmosphere. Thought has power, not only over our own bodies, but very possibly upon the world around us. Shakespeare was right: "There are more things in heaven and earth, Horatio, than are dreamt of in your [and our!] philosophy."

I am especially drawn to Alexander's emphasis on the head's upward movement, in part because my early ballet training makes that a habit easily reclaimed. I know that when I stand like that, I feel lighter in both body and spirit. I know that God is not "up there," but the upward pull serves as a metaphor for a force other than that of gravity: "You have made me for Yourself, and my heart is restless until I rest in You." No wonder medieval artists were so fond of painting the ascension of Jesus, sometimes with only his feet visible as he disappeared into the clouds. We are earth-creatures, yes, but in our hearts, we know that this is not where we belong forever. How else to describe that but "up"?

STRENGTH TRAINING

When our children were young, we would spend long summer afternoons at a community swimming pool complex at the edge of our town. I'd take along a book, bask in the sun, play with the children in the water, and swim a few laps every now and then.

One day, the mother of one of our younger son's friends informed me, "David does eighteen laps a day." Believe it or not, despite my enjoyment of swimming, it had never occurred to me to swim longer than the time it took to cool down in the pool after sitting in the sun. David's mother's boast initiated a conversion for me. Suddenly, I turned around (conversion literally means "go in the other direction") and changed from being a "cool-off" swimmer to a lap swimmer.

I noticed immediately that the exercise made me feel better. But it was the grocery bags that brought to my attention one of the most welcome side-effects of my conversion.

Our driveway paralleled the side porch of our Victorian house, which had no garage. Every time I returned home from grocery shopping, I had to haul the groceries for a family of four from the trunk of the car to the kitchen. There were two routes, neither of which was easy. One involved crossing the porch, opening the front door, going down the hall to the dining room, then into the kitchen. The other entailed walking along a flagstone path to the far side of the back of the house and climbing several steps up to the back door. By the time I deposited the last bag on the kitchen table, my arms ached.

One day, in the middle of the summer of my conversion to lap-swimming, I suddenly realized that my packages were getting lighter. Of course, my packages weighed the same—it was my arms that were getting stronger!

Swimming laps was my introduction to strength training, which is based on the fact that stressing muscles makes them stronger. Physiologists would say that muscles need some "overload." Perhaps you are more familiar with the opposite experience: lack of use weakens the body. If you have ever been confined to bed for a few days, you may have felt a few years older when you first began to move around.

The activity that comes to most people's minds when they hear "strength training" is lifting weights. Indeed, lifting weights is a way to become stronger, and, because strong muscles produce a shapelier body, classes in this activity are sometimes called "body-sculpting." A similar activity is provided by machines like Nautilus, in which the weights are arranged in such a way that they help you to isolate the movement of each part of the body in turn and provide increasing resistance as you move.

But there are other ways to grow stronger. When I swam in the municipal pool, my muscles became stronger because of the resistance of the water as I pushed against it to propel myself in the Australian crawl. You can use your own body's weight for resistance: a familiar example is the push-up, in which you lie on your stomach and try to push the whole weight of your body from the floor with your arms. Earlier, I mentioned an excellent addition to the repertoire of fitness: a long stretchy piece of elastic called a theraband, which comes in different degrees of elasticity and provides resistance as you move. Exercise physiologists recommend using a medium to strong theraband for strength training. Therabands exercise the muscles in a manner similar to free weights like dumbbells, giving a challenge to the muscles through their reluctance to stretch rather than through their weight. For those who want to take their fitness regimes on the road as they travel, they are much easier to pack than dumbbells!

Some forms of exercise incorporate strength training: bicycling for the legs, especially the quadriceps muscles at the front of the thigh; cross-country skiing for both legs and arms; and hatha yoga and Pilates movements in which you push your body weight from the floor.

Many activities of daily life—chopping firewood, pushing a lawnmower, scrubbing the kitchen floor—stress the muscles so that they become stronger. Some people have strength training built into their daily work, judging from the musculature of tree surgeons, construction workers, and other people whose daily work involves physical labor.

We can be imaginative about ways to pursue this goal. My favorite form of strength training during his first year involved a free weight named Gabriel. When he was an infant, he was easy to lift and to hold as we engaged in one of our favorite activities together: dancing to music in the kitchen. Gradually, as he gained weight, I noticed the increased effort I had to expend when I lifted and held him. By the time he was a year old, I came to the realization that I might need to work with some other free weights between visits if we were to keep this up. I needed, in other words, some "overload" in my exercise. This cardinal principle of strength training is a way of saying that my body systems must be challenged beyond their normal capacity—performing the activity for longer periods, more frequently, or with greater intensity—in order to produce improvement.

Strength training is especially important as we grow older, because the mere process of aging can gradually deprive us of strength. But young or old, the fact is that we lose strength rapidly when our exercise or activity is halted.

Our spirits, as well, need challenging in order to remain strong. Often life itself provides us with these challenges. "Life is difficult," writes Scott Peck in *The Road Less Traveled*. "Once we truly know that life is difficult—once we truly understand and accept it—then life is no longer difficult."[13] The best way to explain this sentence is through an example. When I was a student chaplain in a hospital at the edge of Harlem, I learned a great deal about strength from a particular group of patients: elderly, often indigent African-American women. These women had suffered much hardship in their lives, but it had seasoned rather than embittered them, for because of their socio-economic class they had never expected that life would be easy. Rather than complaining about their illness, like a couple of the more privileged patients I visited, or believing it was a punishment from God, they would tell me they knew the "Good Lord" was with them, helping them to persevere.

What about the privileged few to whom life has offered few hardships? The great spiritual traditions teach us that we become stronger by making choices based on what is true and just, rather than always seeking our own comfort. Such choices challenge our self-indulgent selves and help form us as people of integrity. This does not happen overnight: such strength grows in us through a lifetime of work.

One tool for spiritual strength training is regular self-examination. When I was introduced to the practice as a teenager by our parish priest, I thought that self-examination was primarily about sinful actions. That is very likely true at the beginning of our moral formation, as it helps to form us as ethical human beings. As we grow and mature, however, self-examination helps us to look beyond sinful actions to the human weakness at their roots, and reminds us to draw our strength from God.

The results of both physical and spiritual strength training are cumulative and extend over a lifetime. What more efficient way to grow in both bodily and spiritual strength than to combine the two in prayer? I know a priest who performs each of his exercises with free weights fourteen times, while he meditates upon the fourteen Stations of the Cross, beginning with Jesus' being condemned to death by Pilate, and ending with Jesus' body being lowered from the cross. If you lift weights, you can lift intercessions at the same time, thinking of specific people who are in need. When your muscles engage, whether by pushing your own body weight against the wall or the floor, by stretching a theraband, through lifting free weights, or on an exercise machine, you can use that sense of effort to send prayer energy in any direction that it is needed. You might also want to use a mantra, such as "be strong in the faith" or "thine is the kingdom and the power and the glory"; or to use a psalm verse, such as "God is the strength of my life; of whom then shall I be afraid?" (Ps. 27:1).

The following exercises for strengthening the arms provide three examples of providing resistance—your own weight, a theraband, and free weights—all of which can easily be used at home. To use exercise machines like Nautilus for strength training, most of us will have to go to a gym or health club, and will also need to seek some guidance from a trainer. But the exercises below may motivate you to explore strength training further in this way, if you have not done it already.

In performing these exercises, be sure not to hold your breath. If we do not breathe as we are stressing the muscles, we cannot send enough oxygen to them. Our blood pressure may even increase. This is a physical reminder that it is not merely our own effort that strengthens us. It is the breath of life—God's breath—coursing through our bodies and our spirits that enables us to persevere.

Over time, the muscles can be gradually challenged by increasing either the repetitions of the exercise or the weight load. You can standing further away from the wall in the wall push-up, choose a stronger theraband or stand further away from the doorknob to which it is attached, or work with a heavier free weight. The important thing is to succeed in doing the movement correctly. Begin modestly, and then build up your strength.

Your body weight. To experience how it feels to use your own body weight to strengthen your muscles, try this version of the push-up. Stand an arm's length away from a wall and place the palms of your hands on the wall at shoulder level. Inhale. Tighten your abdominal muscles, thinking of pulling the navel toward the spine. Keeping the back of your body—neck, spine, and backs of the legs—as straight as possible, exhale and slowly lean into your hands, trying to keep your elbows close to your sides rather than allowing them to bend outward. Then, as you inhale, push outward again until your body is straight. Repeat this movement eight to fifteen times, or until you reach a point when your muscles rebel at performing it properly.

As you become stronger, you can stand farther away from the wall, so that your beginning position, rather than vertical upright, will be at an angle. This will further tax the muscles.

A variation of this exercise: Stand with the feet and hips sideways to the wall, twisting only at the waist to place your hands on the wall as before. Lean your weight into the wall and push it back from the wall. Repeat this movement until the muscles tire, then switch sides.

A theraband. Take a theraband and loop it around the far side of the doorknob of a door that can be securely closed. The ends of the theraband should be the same length. Now close the door, making sure that the theraband avoids the metal latch and both ends hang outside the door.

Facing the door, grasp one of the ends of the theraband in your right hand. It may be helpful to wind the theraband around your hand in order to keep a tight grip. Back up until the theraband is taut, and inhale. Now, exhaling and keeping your elbow at your side, bend the arm at the elbow and bring the theraband up to your shoulder; inhale and bring your hand back down slowly. Repeat until the muscles tire.

Repeat the exercise with the left arm.

Beginning in the identical position, grasp the theraband with your right hand and take a short step to your left. Now, keeping the arm straight, pull the theraband straight back past the right side of your body. Repeat until the muscles tire.

Repeat the exercise with the left arm.

Free weights. These can be dumbbells of various weights, or, if you have no dumbbells and want to get the feel of using free weights, you can look in your pantry. I've found that two 29-ounce cans of tomato sauce can act as convenient stand-ins.

Hold a weight in each hand, with your arms down to the sides and palms of the hands facing forward. Inhale. Then exhale and bring the weights up toward your shoulders, as in the first theraband exercise. Inhale and bring them slowly back down to your sides.

With your feet slightly apart, hold a weight in each hand at your sides. Inhale. Then, exhaling and keeping your arms straight, lift the dumbbells until they are slightly above your shoulders. Slowly lower the dumbbells to your side as you inhale. This exercise always feels to me like preparing my "wings" so that someday I can actually fly!

How do your arms feel after these exercises? The increased circulation in your arms caused by challenging their strength probably gives your muscles a feeling of melting warmth. If you have not stressed these muscles recently, they may even be sore tomorrow. Stress, whether physical or spiritual, can feel temporarily uncomfortable. "Life is difficult," but when we accept its difficulty life can also be our teacher, like a trainer at the gym who teaches us to persevere and to breathe as we grow in strength of body, mind, and spirit. Strength training, whether provided by life or by weight-bearing exercise, embodies a variation on the ancient prayer for the service of confirmation: "Strengthen us, O God, with your Holy Spirit; empower us for your service, and sustain us all the days of our life."

✳

AEROBIC EXERCISE

At one time in my suburban hometown, when we saw people walking we assumed that their cars were in the repair shop. If you were driving by friends who had the bad fortune to be on foot, it was considered good etiquette to stop your car and offer a ride. Thanks to increasing awareness about fitness for everyone, not merely athletes, things have changed drastically in recent years. Sidewalks and streets are full of walkers and joggers, especially on weekends, going about their business of building and maintaining a healthy cardiovascular system. A parkway that runs along the edge of my hometown is now closed from ten to two on Sundays, enabling bicycle riding—and tricycle and "big wheels" riding—as well as jogging.

As far as I can learn, exercise for the sake of physical prowess probably originated in ancient Greece. There was the courier who collapsed after running on foot in heavy armor to bring the message of the Greek victory over the Persians at Marathon, giving us the word for a long-distance race. But, above all, in the second century B.C.E., the Greeks organized the Olympic Games. The public display of male physical fitness was a high value in classical Greece, assuming the handsome sculptures from that period reflect reality. Some of the events in which naked athletes competed are still familiar to us—running, wrestling, boxing, javelin, and discus. We fortunately no longer have to witness the violence of the chariot race, the *hoplitodromia,* a four-hundred-yard sprint in full armor, or the *pankration,* a savage all-out brawl where eye gouging was the only banned tactic. Nor are we required to exercise naked, unless we choose to skinny-dip.

While we may not be competitive athletes like those who have taken part in the Olympic Games over the centuries, most of us have had the experience of feeling better after exercise that has challenged our hearts to beat faster and our lungs to inhale more oxygen. In the "Breathing" section at the beginning of this chapter, I spoke of our cells' vital need for oxygen. It is the heart muscles that propel this oxygen through the body. The heart contracts rhythmically to send the oxygen-containing blood first into the large artery called the aorta, and then through progressively smaller vessels until the blood finally arrives at the capillaries, where it nourishes the tissues and collects waste products.

The vigor with which the heart accomplishes its work depends on our activity level. When we are resting, our bodies remove about thirty percent of the oxygen from the blood; but during physical exertion, the working muscles and other tissues can consume over seventy-five percent of the blood's oxygen. When we are at rest, each heartbeat sends about two ounces of blood into the aorta; when we exercise, the heart pumps about four ounces of blood per beat and the rate of the heartbeat is also increased. Is it any wonder that we feel better after exercising?

Aerobic capacity is the ability of the heart and blood vessels to deliver oxygen to working muscles. That capacity is enhanced through exercise that increases both the heart rate and the amount of oxygen we are breathing, which is why people speak of a "target" heart rate for such exercise. The formula for arriving at this optimum number is based on subtracting between fifteen and thirty percent from the maximal heart rate for your age. This rate can be calculated by subtracting a woman's age from 210 and a man's from 220, although I have to confess that I don't worry about doing the math. The one time I tried to reach my peak heart rate on an exercise bicycle that recorded it digitally, I couldn't manage to get it up to that point no matter how energetically I pedaled. I know, however, when my lungs and heart have had a good workout, because my chest cavity always feels more spacious afterward, as if the extra air inside it had caused it to expand. A friend who lived for three years with her family in London, on the other hand, said she regularly reached her peak heart rate by hauling her children's clothing from the basement laundry of their tall London townhouse to their rooms nestled under the rooftop. Such exercise strengthens the collaborative work of the heart and lungs, and it is one of the major ways we can help to keep ourselves healthy throughout life.

When we are challenged by situations that threaten or frighten us, our body responds by what scientists call the "fight or flight" response, in which the adrenaline that is released prepares us to either flee or fight by quickening our heartbeat, breathing, and muscular readiness. While there are many good suggestions for stress reduction through relaxation, breathing, and meditation, another option is just to *use* the adrenaline surge for something beneficial. That could be anything from a long, vigorous walk in the woods to digging out a compost heap or scrubbing a bathtub. When we *use* stress rather than reducing it, we are avoiding some of the damage that this hyper-ready physical state can do if it has no outlet.

On the other hand, feeling stress because we are trying to accomplish a goal while exercising can have adverse results. Researchers at Harvard have discovered that an overly competitive attitude toward exercise can stimulate the release of stress hormones into the blood stream. Apparently, it is healthier to exercise for the sake of exercising, rather than to do so with a competitive spirit.

It is generally agreed that for cardiovascular fitness we should spend twenty to thirty minutes three or four times a week in dynamic aerobic exercise. Tried and true examples include swimming, walking, jogging, aerobic dancing, cross-country skiing, and cycling. If it is bad weather, or if you prefer them, exercise machines can take the place of outdoor exercise. My husband and I have a Nordic Track for that purpose, which not only strengthens our arms and our legs but also gives us a good cardiovascular workout. Any gym or health club offers an array of devices that enable you to pedal, jog, or climb stairs, without getting anywhere!

You should ease into each exercise session, slowly increasing your intensity as you warm up. Our garage and driveway automatically provide such warm-ups for us. After we have maneuvered our bikes out of the garage, following the narrow route between the recycling bins and our car, we coast down the driveway, then turn right onto our street and slowly increase our speed until we reach the bike trail that leads to the little town to the west. In the winter, we take down our cross-country skis, which have waited patiently on the rack in the garage until the first snowfall, and lace up our ski boots, giving our backs a good stretch. We glide down the sloped driveway, cross the street gingerly, and slip through the gap in the golf course hedge, conveniently located just across from us. Then, the serious exercise begins.

Afterward, there is the need to cool down. Experts advise that we should keep moving around for at least ten minutes after sustained exertion, making it easier for the blood that has been fueling the muscles to return to the heart. Should you remain stationary, blood can pool in the veins. Moving around not only prevents this, but helps the body to remove metabolic wastes and to dissipate heat.

In a special way, aerobic exercise illumines the metaphor of breath as prayer. As we expand our physical lungs, so we can expand our "spiritual" lungs through the abundant oxygen of God's presence. For centuries, monastics and clergy have done that through the daily offices: services of worship at regular intervals during the day. Some of the rest of us also find that daily fixed periods of prayer help keep us "aerobically fit" spiritually. But there are other ways of increasing our capacity for God's presence as well. The contemplative who spends time in silence with God in the morning and then dwells in that center of presence and inner calm for the rest of day is one example. The person who "breathes out" energy while doing God's work in the world, serving the poor or working for peace and justice, is doing another form of aerobic exercise. The artist whose work flows from "inspiration"—yet another breath word—breathes out through music, words, dance, or images a unique offering of prayer.

Furthermore, the heart—not merely the organ but the symbolic center of our emotions—grows stronger as it is challenged. Life itself gives us frequent opportunities for "spiritual aerobics," both through enduring our own suffering and involving ourselves with the suffering of others. Confronting fear helps us develop courage (literally *coeurage*, *heart*-ness). Persevering in difficult tasks provides greater inner stamina.

Aerobic exercise can be combined seamlessly with breathing the life and renewal of prayer into our lives. Let me give you some examples from my own experience, hoping that they will inspire your own ideas. The repetitive, almost hypnotic motions of some aerobic exercise can induce in me a feeling of energy and happiness. Sometimes I just savor the experience. At other times, a mantra such as the phrase "fully alive" comes to me like a gift. Often, as my mind floats free, I become more fully in touch with my own unconscious, intuitive thought, which is a way that I believe God speaks to us.

Sometimes I use aerobic exercise to work off—or perhaps more accurately, "pray off"—an emotion like anger, fear, or disappointment. Swimming, which challenges the whole body, is especially effective for this task. Somehow, the support of the water makes it feel like a safe place to process these feelings, as if one were literally swimming in the ocean of God's acceptance and love.

Finally, because I have a weak memory for numbers and have trouble when swimming to remember how many laps I have finished, I have devised an alternative system. I begin with three laps, in the name of the Trinity. Then I swim my intercessions. I arrange them in groups of six, so that I will remember them. First come my loved ones, next others who are in special need. On some days I swim for the health of earth, air, water, and the creatures of this planet. I swim for a cessation of war and violence. If some concern seems especially urgent, I will add a lap or two on its behalf. Needless to say, if I were to cover all the needs of the world, I would still be swimming many hours later. But at least it is a beginning.

Set aside at least twenty minutes and go out for a brisk walk. Warm up by strolling at a relaxed pace for a few minutes, then increase your tempo. Notice the pace of your breath and silently repeat the words "fully alive" to synchronize with its rhythm. If another word comes to you while you are walking, you can change your mantra. You may want to use the word "God" or "Jesus," or even the Hebrew word for breath, *nuach*. Perhaps the thought of friends in need of your prayer will come to you, and you will use their names. Perhaps you will even find yourself so happy to be moving that you just focus on the breath, reveling in the feeling of being "fully alive." Cool down by moving more slowly for a few minutes.

Take some time afterward to observe how your body—and your spirit—feel. Finally, breathe a prayer of gratitude to God for your life, and the wondrous efficiency and complexity of your body.

Of all the kinds of exercise we include in our daily lives, aerobic exercise is perhaps the most necessary for our continued well-being. But it is time-consuming. It is tempting to feel there is not time for it, just as it is tempting to feel there is not time for prayer.

The solution? Andrew of Crete thought of it in the eighth century, although he had never heard of aerobic exercise: "While I breathe I pray!"

✳

DANCE

"Thump, thump, *thump,* thump." That sound introduced the PBS series on the history of music hosted by the violinist Yehudi Menuhin. *"Thump,* thump, *thump,* thump." Then Menuhin's voice could be heard about that insistent rhythm: "The mother's heartbeat remains deep within long after we emerge into the light of day, imprinted on us like our identity. We feel its loss and must replace it with other sounds. . . . Just as the involuntary heartbeat produces life's first rhythm, so music gives back to us the pulse of life."[14]

I remember as a little girl putting my ear against my mother's chest to hear that *"thump,* thump, *thump,* thump." Later, my feet would create those primal rhythms as, along with the other children in a preschool dancing class, I rediscovered an elemental pleasure in my body becoming one with the music. I relived this experience many years later, when I myself became a teacher of creative movement. In every class of two-year-olds there would be at least one child who would stand up and bounce up and down, bending her knees to the pulse of the music. One I know even began dancing at seven months, before he was able to stand. He would sit on the floor, knees turned in and feet out (the inverse of the lotus position), and bounce, with a blissful expression on his face, whenever he heard music. Perhaps he had gotten an extraordinarily early start because his mother was a professional cellist and he had spent the nine months before birth only an inch or so away from her instrument.

One of the reasons I loved to teach creative movement to young children was that it gave me the freedom to dance spontaneously myself. The structure of ballet classes over the years had provided my body with a movement vocabulary and a technique. Through ballet I had learned many things that have come in handy throughout life, including discipline, hard work, and the ability to work through physical discomfort rather than trying to avoid it. I learned the importance of first mentally picturing the way I would move, before I began to dance the steps a teacher demonstrated. I am grateful for this training in watching a combination (or series of steps) and imprinting it in my own body so that I can perform it myself. I am sure that it helps to keep my brain youthful—somewhat like crossword puzzles for the body! Long ago I discovered that when a combination was especially challenging, if I imagined myself dancing, not as myself but as some much more accomplished dancer—say, Margot Fonteyn—some of the difficulty slipped away. I do not know how this worked, but it did—and does. The imagination is a powerful ally when our bodies are challenged.

Ballet classes continue to be an ascetical discipline for me, teaching me about perseverance in the face of difficulty, like the images in 2 Timothy of "fighting the good fight" and "finishing the race." They teach me humility, for, especially as I age, the goals in this art are unattainable. This is true in music, and perhaps theater as well: ask any professional in the performing arts if they are ever totally satisfied with their performances. Dancing also involves using an art form in order to remain fit: a winning combination!

Modern dance, which is more akin to the creative movement classes I taught, is a forum for other kinds of learning. As the body learns to interpret themes and express emotions, the spirit is freed as well. The mother of such freedom is Isadora Duncan, who wrote about her work in the early twentieth century: "I am inspired by the movement of the trees, the waves, the snows, by the connection between passion and the storm, between the breeze and gentleness. . . . I always put into my movements a little of that divine continuity which gives to all of Nature its beauty and life."[15] I like to think that Isadora should be hailed as a muse of the environmental movement, helping us to connect viscerally with the world of nature in which human society is embedded.

The great dance pioneer Martha Graham used her freedom from set dance forms to plumb the depths of the human heart and psyche. One of her earliest and most personal dances, "Lamentation," a study of a grief-stricken woman costumed in a tube of fabric, is said to have helped one member of the audience finally to face her own grief, allowing her to weep for the first time since a tragic loss.

We may not be Martha Grahams, but our own improvisational dance can be healing for us as individuals, as it allows us to process dilemmas, disappointments, both physical and spiritual discomfort, and fear, as we "think" and "feel" with our bodies.

There will be more about that later in this book, when we explore how movement can be a form of reflective prayer.

Dance takes many shapes. Some people enjoy the sociability of folk dancing, square dancing, and contra dancing, surely outward and visible signs of the fact of human community. In the contra dancing sessions in our town, Democrats dance the patterns with Republicans, old with young, college professors with blue collar workers, to say nothing of the various shades of skin color represented. Perhaps it would be fruitful to offer contra dancing during the coffee breaks at the United Nations, or the United States Congress.

We can also learn much from participating in the unique ethnic dances of other peoples. I remember been energized by the strong movements of African dance, which pervades every facet of traditional tribal life. When my church musician husband used to moonlight by playing the organ in a nearby synagogue, I looked forward to the receptions that followed solemn services such as *bat* and *bar mitzvot,* for they inevitably included Israeli dancing. The rabbi was always amused to see a clerical collar moving among the revelers. My Indian godchild Angela, who studied Indian classical dance, taught me a few graceful hand movements from that discipline. All of these experiences have helped me know another group of people a little bit better.

Some of the first dates my husband and I had were at Arthur Murray's Ballroom Dance studio: Bob had won six free lessons by correctly answering a question like, "On what side of the U. S. border did the Rumba originate?" during a telephone quiz. Those were the days of dancing together, of course, with the man leading and the woman following. I had been fairly proficient when I was in high school, before I had gone back to ballet classes, but now as a trained dancer it was difficult for me to follow a partner. As we practiced the variations of the fox trot or waltz I gradually caught on, and learned to respond to the gentle pressure of Bob's hand on my back, guiding me in the patterns we had learned. I like to think that the sensitivity that was needed for each of us to dance as partners contributed not a little bit to our long marriage.

I remember one particular day in my life that I did not have the heart to dance. I was supposed to go to ballet class on November 23, 1964, the day after John F. Kennedy was shot. This unthinkable event was to people of my generation what 9/11 is to the world today, and, heavy in body and spirit, I could not bring myself to even enter the dance studio. I felt like my three-year-old dance student who declined to join the other children in the class because she was felt worried about being displaced by her newborn baby brother: "I can't dance, because I'm sad." Dancing usually takes a certain lightness of heart.

But it can also give us a lightness of heart. Dancing can reassure us—at least through our bodies—that in the long run there is hope that goodness will prevail. The Trappist monk and author Thomas Merton writes:

> For the world and time are the dance of the Lord in emptiness. The silence of the spheres is the music of a wedding feast. The more we persist in misunderstanding the phenomena of life, the more we analyze them out into strange finalities and complex purposes of our own, the more we involve ourselves in sadness, absurdity and despair. But it does not matter much, because no despair of ours can alter the reality of things, or stain the joy of the cosmic dance which is always there.[16]

In his journey through the afterlife, Dante encounters dancing not in hell nor in purgatory, but in paradise. There, the Dominicans and Franciscans, who were enemies during Dante's lifetime, "match motion to motion and song with song" as they circle and dance "with light joyful and gracious."

When we do not have the heart to join the "cosmic dance" or when the dancers of Dante's paradise seem illusory, there is one Partner who gives us the heart to move in God's choreography, rather than to sit on the sidelines of life:

> I danced in the morning when the world was begun,
> And I danced in the moon and the stars and the sun,
> And I came down from heaven and I danced on the earth;
> At Bethlehem I had my birth.
> Dance then, wherever you may be
> *I am the Lord of the dance, said he,*
> *And I'll lead you all, wherever you may be,*
> *And I'll lead you all in the dance, said he.*[17]

St. Francis of Assisi wrote a poem called the "Canticle of the Sun," in which the sun, moon, stars, wind, water, fire, and earth praise God. Play some music that expresses this theme for you. Perhaps it will be the hymn "All Creatures of Our God and King," found in many hymnals, a part of the "Missa Gaia" or "Earth Mass" of Paul Winter, or an upbeat jazz or classical music composition.

Now dance the "qualities" of each of the elements in the "Canticle of the Sun." If the sun were to dance, how would it move? Would your arms and hands become the rays, stretching throughout space? Would you bend sideways like a crescent moon, move lightly like a twinkling star, whirl like the wind, move fluidly like water, jump with the energy of a blazing fire, and finally kneel on the earth?

These are just suggestions: feel free to improvise your own movements. You can also add your own subject matter. St. Francis, despite his fabled affinity with animals, did not mention them in his poem. This improvisation can be done in any space you have available. If it is a very small space, you can even just move your arms and hands.

This improvisation may take you back to childhood dance classes. It also takes us back in history, for at the dawn of dance history, all dance was a sacred celebration of creation, an expression of the divine.

✳

"HOME WORK"

When our children were small and I spent most of my time at home, I adopted as my patron saint the monastery cook Brother Lawrence. He gave me something to aim for:

> The time of business does not with me differ from the time of prayer; and in the noise and clutter of my kitchen, while several persons [read "children"] are at the same time calling for different things, I possess God in as great tranquillity as if I were upon my knees at the blessed sacrament.

I have a waterstained edition, dated 1895, of the little book *The Practice of the Presence of God,* a collection of conversations with Brother Lawrence recorded by a seventeenth-century admirer. The foreword by Hannah Whitall Smith, although written over a century ago for readers of this edition, still rings true:

> This little book. . . seems to me one of the most helpful I know. It fits into the lives of all human beings, let them be rich or poor, learned or unlearned, wise or simple. The woman at her wash-tub, or the stone-breaker on the road, can carry on the "practice" here taught with as much ease and as much assurance of success as the priest at his altar or the missionary in his field of work.

Automatic washing machines may have replaced wash-tubs, and heavy equipment may have made the work of building roads easier, but most of us still need on occasion to do some manual labor. The work we do, whether of earning a living or maintaining a home, can become, Brother Lawrence tells us, a way of prayer, as valid as the chants reverberating in the monastery chapel where his more educated brethren sang the Daily Office.

Although the women's movement came along just as I was beginning married life and I welcomed its vision of new freedom and opportunity, I always resisted some of its initial denigration of domesticity. In fact, I seriously considered writing an alternative book to Betty Friedan's *Feminine Mystique* called *The Feminine Mystic,* proposing the tending of home and hearth as a way to draw closer to God. Especially when my professional work has been open-ended and unpredictable, as is often the case both in teaching and ministry, it is a comfort to spend a day creating order and harmony in our home. The results of folding the laundry, scrubbing the kitchen floor, or cleaning the basement, although temporary, are tangible and immediate, unlike the results of introducing preschoolers to dance and music or counseling a parishioner.

When, because of the pressure of other duties or fatigue, I feel reluctant to undertake some necessary physical work, a change of attitude can transform it. The wife of a bishop I know confessed that she always hated to vacuum until she realized that the vacuum cleaner created wonderful "white noise" that drowned out not only the extraneous city noises outside her windows, but the telephone as well, and she used this newfound "silence" in order to pray as she worked.

I need only walk out our back door to find a whole world of exercise and prayer possibilities in the garden, because the metaphor of gardening is such a congenial way to speak of things of the spirit. The sometimes arduous physical work of digging, pruning, and pushing a heavy wheelbarrow full of compost challenges my body as it feeds my spirit. One of our sons makes a livelihood tending the garden in an environmental community in Oregon, as well as teaching visiting apprentices about organic gardening methods. Because he is also editor of the community's magazine and often writes about his manual labor, his readers can testify to the fact that this regular work develops an integrated spirituality.

Some people choose to do physical work as a hobby in their free time because it satisfies them spiritually. One clergywoman I know shared with me that she would like to make her passion for knitting a true vocation, and she now is leading workshops about how the "click click" of knitting needles can be a prayer, as well as an enacted reflection on the interweaving of the events and people in our lives. I have friends whose most authentic prayer happens as they knead and bake fresh loaves of bread, as a "fragrant offering" to God. Especially for those of us who work mostly in our "heads," we feel more human, more connected in bodyspirit when we work with our hands. I know that after finishing this manuscript I will head either for the garden, the ironing board, or the vacuum cleaner!

We are fortunate to have as neighbors in our town many people who make their living through physical labor. We enjoy the company of our contractor and his sons (one of whom whistles as he works), who come to do odd jobs beyond our skills. We have gotten to know our articulate tree surgeon, our soft-spoken plumber, and the thoughtful owner and employees of the heating and cooling service who successfully used our home as a test run for installing their very first geothermal system. To a person, these all regard their work not merely as a means of earning money, but as their passion. Like the physician we all wish we had, they take plenty of time to tell us things: what might improve the drainage around our house, or the several options in treating an ailing tree. Dorothy Sayers would approve. The church, she writes, should be telling the carpenter, for example, that "the first demand that his religion makes upon him is that he make good tables.... No crooked table-legs or ill-fitting drawers, ever, I dare swear, came out of the carpenter's shop at Nazareth."[18]

Then there are those whose physical work is that of creating beauty and meaning. They use their bodies as the instruments of their art. We hear their exercise, made audible, when we pass the Conservatory in town—the five-finger exercises of the pianists, the bowed scales of the violinists, the vocalizations of the singers. Should we be able to look in the third-story windows of the ballet studio in town, we would see exercise made visible in *pliés, tendus,* and *grands battements.* We can run our hands over an outdoor sculpture of Martin Luther King in one of our public parks: exercise made tangible.

It is interesting to note that the revered Mohandas Gandhi, the leader of the Indian nationalist movement, began a program of hand spinning and weaving. The purpose was not only to aid India's economic freedom through cloth production, or its political freedom through challenging the British textile industry, but to promote social freedom through the dignity of labor. The dignity of labor! Our homes may be filled with "labor-saving" devices, but physical work provides a satisfaction that can be found in no other way.

Every time I made a pastoral visit to Marjorie, who was in her nineties, she would smile and give me a potholder or dishcloth that she had crocheted. One of the most difficult passages in her last years was when she could no longer see to do this work.

She spoke of feeling "useless." In her eyes, her dignity was gone—although, of course, it was not gone, either in God's eyes or mine.

Despite the story in Genesis that suggests that the necessity for physical work was punishment for Adam's sin—"cursed is the ground because of you; in toil you shall eat of it. . . . By the sweat of your face you shall eat bread"—physical labor need not be merely a burden that we wish we could avoid. It can be spiritual exercise. Even those activities that seem most ordinary can go through the metamorphosis suggested in the pastor-poet George Herbert's poem "The Elixir," in which he tells us that it is our attitude that makes the difference. Our working "before God" is like the longed-for "philosopher's stone" of alchemy that, once found, would be able to transform even the basest metals into gold:

> Teach me, my God and King,
>   In all things thee to see,
> And what I do in anything,
> To do it as for thee. . . .
>
>   All may of thee partake;
>   Nothing can be so mean,
> Which with this tincture (for thy sake)
> Will not grow bright and clean.
>
>   A servant with this clause
>   Makes drudgery divine;
> Who sweeps a room, as for thy laws
> Makes that and th' action fine.
>
>   This is the famous stone
>   That turneth all to gold;
> For that which God doth touch and own
> Cannot for less be told.[19]

One of the gifts of the Celtic spiritual tradition is the practice of invoking divine protection in the activities of daily life. Many collections of Celtic prayers and invocations are available, most of them originally collected by the scholar Alexander

Carmichael in the nineteenth century. Nothing was too ordinary to be included in prayer. The woman kindled her fire in the morning "in presence of the holy angels of heaven" and prayed over the loom on which she was to weave the family's garments: "Bless, O Chief of generous chiefs, My loom and everything a-near me." Her husband sowed the seed in the field "in name of Him who gave it growth," and when he sent out his cattle to graze prayed for "the friendship of God the Son to bring you home."

A few days after returning from the Scottish island of Iona, where I encountered so many examples of this Celtic spirit, I found myself standing in front of a sink full of dirty dishes, wishing I could be anywhere else. Suddenly, I remembered my Celtic forbears and found myself saying silently, "Bless, O Holy Trinity, my cleaning of these pots and pans." Needless to say, the burdensome task became much lighter—in fact, almost a pleasure, as I smiled to myself at imagining I was a Scottish housewife more than a century ago.

Choose a day during which you will try to remember the invocations of the Celtic housewife and her farmer husband, especially when you find yourself resisting a task. You might even bless your grocery shopping: "Creator of all that nourishes us, you give to us the needs of the body." In the office, before you have to write a report you have been dreading, you can silently intone, "Bless to me, O God, each word that my fingers type." If you have to get into the car for yet another errand, the task may become less onerous if you pray, "Bless to me, O God, the path whereon I go." It is not only entertaining to create these colorful small prayers, but it can do more than anything else I have tried to change my attitude!

CHAPTER 3

PRAYING THROUGH
THE BODY

THE SCENE IS a monastery chapel; the liturgy is the life-profession of a monk. This day is the culmination of a long process of discernment that began several years ago. The monk and the community have come to the decision that he does indeed have a vocation to the vowed religious life.

The words and the music of the liturgy are impressive, but what I remember is neither of these. Instead, I remember the moment when the monk prostrated himself face down before the altar, full length on the floor, with arms outstretched. Never before had I seen such a dramatic example of praying through the body.

In chapter two I suggested ways in which various forms of physical exercise can be transformed so that they become part of your spiritual practice. In this chapter we will look at things the other way around: how can our *prayer* be expressed through the use of our *bodies,* as illustrated by the prostrate monk?

In suggesting some answers to this question, I hope that, whether you pray with words, through thought, or in simple stillness, your prayer will be enriched by including your body. For some, these exercises will have the effect of deepening all of their prayer, even when they are sitting quietly in a pew at church. Others may discover that movement itself is their most congenial way of praying.

In the following section, for convenience, I have divided ways of praying into three categories, something I do not like to do! To systematize prayer in this way is artificial, because our relationship with God is ideally one of freedom and spontaneity. I am always reminded of John Donne's sonnet "at the round earth's imagined corners," for, even in his day, people rarely traveled in straight lines, due north or east or south or west, but followed the contours of the land. In the same way, each category of prayer usually contains elements of the others.

Some of the following suggestions for praying through the body can apply to prayer in groups and can even be used in worship. But all of them, whether you do them in your living room alone or with other participants at a workshop or Sunday service, have the potential for enriching your own bodyspirit's experience of God.

CONTEMPLATIVE PRAYER

Contemplative prayer, sometimes called centering prayer or meditation, can be described as the prayer of simply being still in God's presence. The stillness in question, however, is not primarily stillness of body: it is the quieting of our busy minds. The buzz that persists when we try to become still has been wryly described as "mosquito mind" or "monkey mind."

A seminary professor of mine once described the process of quieting this annoying buzz. Picture your brain as two television sets, one representing the left hemisphere of your brain and one the right. The controls on the left (the verbal, logical, controlling part of our brain) are set at the highest volume, while the volume in the right hemisphere (the domain of poetry, dream, metaphor, and intuition) is turned very low. The messages of both are being played, but you are unable to hear those of the right hemisphere because of the din of the left. Methods of quieting ourselves for contemplative prayer help us turn the volume down on the blaring left television set, so that we can be present to the still small voice of the right. Most of these methods include focus on our breath; many also include mentally repeating a mantra or focusing on an image.

In Christianity, attention to the body rarely has been included in the effort to quiet ourselves for prayer. An exception is the Hesychast tradition of the Eastern Orthodox Church, which some of us first encountered in reading Salinger's novel *Franny and Zooey*. In an early scene in the novel, Franny tells her boyfriend about the book he has noticed in her handbag, *The Way of the Pilgrim*. It is the journal of a Russian peasant who sets forth on a pilgrimage to find out what the Bible means by "praying without ceasing." He meets a holy man who teaches him the Jesus Prayer: "Lord Jesus Christ, have mercy on me." The pilgrim continues to repeat the Jesus Prayer inwardly, and his breath and even his heartbeat take on the rhythm of the words, reminding him of the abiding presence of God.

Although set in the nineteenth century, *The Way of the Pilgrim* hearkens back to the ancient Eastern Orthodox tradition of Hesychasm associated with monks who lived during the fourth and fifth centuries. These monks taught the technique of sitting with the head bowed, the eyes fixed on the place of the heart, and the breathing adjusted to the rhythm of the Jesus Prayer. This was considered a way to achieve a union of the mind with the "heart"—meaning, in Eastern thought, not just the physical organ or the seat of the emotions, but the whole self: intellect, emotions, and body.

My own attentiveness to my body's weight, reminding me of my earthliness, and to my breath, reminding me of God's gift of life, has become for me a kind of non-verbal Jesus Prayer. Perhaps I am a contemporary version of a Hesychast! It is quite striking how quickly attention to the body and breath quiets the spirit, which is one reason that hatha yoga and similar practices have become so popular in our over-stimulating culture.

There is a simple way to notice the wordless bodyspirit connection in prayer. Take each of the following prayer postures in turn, for five minutes or so. Before you move on to the next one, reflect on how each position of your body has expressed the "feel" of your relationship to God.

1. Kneel with your head bowed and hands clasped.

2. Now, if it is comfortable for you, sit on the floor in a cross-legged posture with your hands on your knees, and breathe quietly.

3. Continue to pray quietly sitting in a chair, with your hands on your lap.

4. Stand with hands raised, palms up, at the level of your shoulders.

5. Begin to walk slowly, as in a meditation walk, keeping a sense of your quiet center as you breathe and move.

Experiment now with noticing that even the position in which you hold your hands changes the way you feel.

1. In hatha yoga, for example, bringing the flat palms together, with the hands pointed upward at chest level, is called the "welcoming the deity" position. We

can see this position echoed in the way Asians often greet one another, bowing with the hands together.

2. Another position, from the Zen tradition, involves nesting one hand, palm up, inside the palm of the other, allowing the tips of the thumbs to touch one another, to represent "the jewel in the hand, opening endlessly."[20]

3. How does it feel when your fists are clenched?

4. How does it feel when you allow them to relax and open?

5. In his book *Praying With Our Hands,* Jon Sweeney writes, "Although we tend to think of the hands as 'parts' of the body, they are in fact no mere appendages; they *embody* the whole human person."[21] To understand the wisdom of this insight, use your hands in the following simple movement prayer. Clench your hands together tightly for a few moments. Then allow them to relax, letting the fingers unfold and open.

I remember loving the childhood game called "Here is the church, here is the steeple, open the door and see all the people." We would interlace our fingers, cupping them inward so they would be hidden in our hands, with only our index fingers for the steeple, and then open our hands inside out to reveal the interlaced fingers. Perhaps this was part of my early training in theology, as well as a childlike "hand-prayer." One church in New York used drawings of this game on its letterhead to illustrate that the church consisted of the people, not the building.

Not only the posture or movement of the body and the hands, but the bodily senses as well can guide us toward the quietness of contemplation. One of the most powerful senses for this purpose is the sense of touch. Prayer beads are used in many traditions to focus on the presence of God. The early followers of Muhammad created strings of thirty-three, sixty-six, and ninety-nine beads with which to pray the names of Allah. Orthodox Christian monks still tie strings of one hundred knots, one for each prayer. The rosaries of both the Roman Catholic and the Anglican traditions are used in this way. Although these all began as a means of "counting" prayers, their use tends to draw the user beyond mere words to a simple attentiveness to God.

Holding one of the rocks I have brought home over the years from holy places such as Canterbury, the Mont-Saint-Michel, or the island of Iona has helped to center my spirit when I have felt especially fragmented. Even an object like a seashell, a feather, a pine cone, or a blade of grass can bring the power of the sense of touch into our prayer life.

The sense of smell is situated in a place in the brain that is very close to the site of our memory, and can evoke places where we have sensed the holy. Incense always reminds me of the Saturdays I spent as a teenager in Manhattan. They began with piano lessons and music theory classes uptown at Juilliard. I would then take the subway or bus downtown, and spend the afternoon at a museum, bookstore, or sometimes standing room at the opera. On the way to Grand Central Terminal to catch the train home, I would usually try to include a visit to the Church of St. Mary the Virgin, where the smell of incense hovered all week long. Merely inhaling the air helped me to feel God's presence.

Hearing and really *listening* to sounds that we like—plainsong, birdsong, Bach, bells—is, paradoxically, a doorway to inner silence for many people. Strangely, even when we are surrounded by background noises that we do *not* like, it is helpful first to listen to them, and then to let them go gently.

Even the sense of taste, whether it be tasting the bread or wine of the Eucharist or a particularly delicious food we associate with a special time in our lives, can be a doorway to prayer. At the end of the Sunday worship at Iona Abbey, each member of the departing congregation is given two small oat cakes and instructed to give one of them to a stranger during the coffee hour afterward. I am sure that now the mere taste of an oatcake will take me back to that extraordinary place.

In this very visual culture, it goes without saying that the sense of sight is a powerful ally in our prayer. For that reason, a friend who runs a retreat program always places an arrangement that might include flowers, vines, stones, fabric, water, icons, or candles in the center of the circle of chairs around her meditation room, helping those of us who come there to pray to first feast our eyes upon beauty.

Christians have learned much about contemplative prayer from other traditions, especially the disciplines that arose in the East, such as Zen Buddhism. I remember my excitement in the 1970s when I came across a little book in a London bookstore entitled *Christian Zen,* written by William Johnston, an Irish Jesuit working in Tokyo. My path was equally enriched by his study *Silent Music,* which juxtaposed eastern and western religious insights with the discoveries of modern science in biofeedback and brainwaves.

He spoke of the healing power of this kind of prayer, which, because it reaches the "unconscious caverns of the mind," can effect a cure that is both physical and psychological. This is true, I believe, because when we "just sit" before God, trying to empty ourselves of our insistent thoughts and desires, we are beginning to find ourselves. By noticing that we are being drawn toward the magnetic field emanating from the center of our planet, we move toward acceptance of our human condition as earth-creatures and begin to pay better attention to our body's needs. As we sit in prayer, each breath that fills our lungs is likely to supply not only our oxygen but also our gratitude for life, flooding our psyches with what some would call "good energy."

Aerobic Exercise

Paradoxically, the *movement* of the body, as well as the immobility of the body that is more customary in centering prayer, can also help take us to these unconscious caverns of the mind, where we can simply be present to God without our unruly thoughts getting in the way. Long-distance runners speak of a "runner's high," and I suspect that they are describing the moments when they move past thinking to simply *being.* This can happen with other aerobic exercise as well, such as swimming, cycling, and cross-country skiing. I remember a "high" like that while cross-country skiing over twenty-five years ago, an extraordinary moment that I tried to recapture in verse:

Bright sun, blue sky, the woods sculptured with snow
  and awhisper with birds—
Four or five miles we had skied, my husband and I.
I was ahead.
"Let's stop and rest."
I paused, closed my eyes, and rested.
The One hidden within was without, also, a blinding presence.
No icy patch, but You, would have knocked me off my feet,
  If he had not said, "Let's go on, now."

When I try to analyze what had happened at that time, I realize that my body had been so occupied in vigorous exercise, breathing the clear air and reveling in the wintry beauty, that my mind could float free of words and ideas. I had become inwardly still, open to the Reality who is always there.

Have there been times when repetitive exercise over a period of time (probably at least forty-five minutes to an hour) has made you feel calm, quiet, and free?

Movement Mantras

The cross-country skiing episode gave me an experience of my mind cleared of thoughts, as if I had completely turned off the left-hand television set. Another way of discovering inner stillness is to tune that "set" to a channel in which there is a repetitive word or phrase to occupy it, through using a verbal mantra—a word or phrase repeated over and over. Many people have discovered the power of adding simple repetitive action to a mantra, so that the movement of the body provides a still stronger focus.

Over the course of history, people have instinctively used such a prayer technique, although they might not have labeled it "movement mantra." I think of davening in the Jewish tradition, a repetitive bowing of the body often done by Jewish worshipers praying at the Holy Wall of the temple in Jerusalem. At the synagogue where my husband used to play the organ, there was once an art exhibit that featured a beautiful articulated sculpture of a rabbi doing just that: when pushed gently, the figure would daven, rocking forward and back. In fact, I sometimes catch myself doing a gentle form of unobtrusive davening by rocking the weight from the front to the back of the feet while I celebrate the Eucharist at the altar. Watch carefully, and you will very likely discover that I am not the only priest who does so.

Movement mantras can be as subtle as my gentle rocking back and forth at the altar or as expansive as the following. I use these movements, celebrating the ways we know God, to begin and end many of the retreats I lead.

Stand, kneel, or sit tall on your chair or on the floor. Inhale and reach upward, silently using whatever word you use for the concept of God as creator and parent—Father, Mother, Abba, Creator, Earth-maker. I think of this as the movement of a toddler asking to be picked up; my inhalation reminds me of the divine gift of life-breath.

Then exhale and open your arms to the side, so that your body is in a cruciform shape, using your word for Jesus—Lord, Christ, God among us. Exhaling reminds me of the self-emptying life of Jesus in which people recognized the fullness of God's unconditional love.

Finally, use your word for the Spirit of God, inhaling and bringing your hands to the center of the chest to represent the Spirit dwelling within you, and then exhaling and reaching forward to represent the Spirit in the world, connecting us to one another. Whether you think "Father, Son, and Holy Spirit, "Abba, Jesu, Spiritu Sancte," or "Creator, Redeemer, Sustainer" does not matter, as the movement represents better than any words the mystery that is the Trinity.

Recordings of the music from the Taizé community in France provide many chants that will give you ideas for movement mantras. I particularly like to use *"Dona nobis pacem, Domine,"* using the sign for "peace" in American Sign Language for the deaf:

Sitting, standing, or kneeling, press your hands together in front of you, first with one hand on top and then with the other hand on top, as if you were pressing cookie dough flat, to signify the kind of stalemate that results in war and violence. Then, turning your palms down, spread out your hands and move them in opposite directions as if you were smoothing out a tablecloth, until your arms are straight. I think "conflict, conflict, resolution" when I do that. I offer to God particular concerns about the violence so rampant in this world as I move this mantra. Sometimes the solutions seem so difficult and so impossible that I need to let my mind rest, and simply let my body do the praying.

A repetitive movement need not be the embodiment of a verbal mantra to become contemplative. A priest I know uses knitting in this way; another spins her prayer. Perhaps you have heard Stanford's *Magnificat in G,* in which Mary, like my friend, sings her song of praise to God to the background rhythm of the spinning wheel. People who are potters tell me that their focus at the wheel centers their spirit, as well as centering the bowl being formed. The closest I have come to experiencing this type of movement mantra is when I discovered that the extremely tedious task of hulling a mountain of gooseberries I had bought at our farmers' market could become prayer, as my busy hands did their task, leaving my mind free to be occupied with God.

For many artists, engaging in their art form is contemplative practice. A watercolor of ocean, sky, and sand by my friend Susan, a hermit and painter, hangs over our mantelpiece. Because it was her prayer, it creates a focal point of calm and piece in our living room. At the piano, I have been practicing Bach's *Goldberg Variations* in order to maintain my musical skills, but I soon discovered that they were spiritual practice as well. I was elated to read in Ralph Kirkpatrick's edition of the work that they were like a rosary, because the styles of the variations occur in cyclical sets of threes: a canon, an independent variation, and an elaborate two-manual arabesque. It was not only because of musical structure that this work has become like a rosary for me, for exploring Bach's beauty and complexity focuses and quiets my mind, and I feel "tuned" after I have spent some time with him. Buddhist monks sometimes enact their prayer by spending hours creating an intricate sand painting. Those fortunate enough to see it marvel and then mourn, as, after it is finished, it is effaced. For the monks, it is the process of creating the painting, not the finished product, that is the prayer.

Improvisation and Ecstasy

When words alone do not suffice, you can improvise movement. I remember making a trip to visit a dying friend one day while I was spending a long weekend at a retreat house. When I returned in the evening, I knew I had to live into my sadness in some way, and asked the guestmaster if I could use the chapel for prayer. Fortunately, the chapel was empty of pews, with only a few chairs around the periphery. I put a Taizé tape into the sound system, and knelt, rocking forward and back, then rising to move around the room to express my crying out to God for my friend.

Similar to that dance in the chapel is the kind of pure movement that is called "ecstatic": it takes you out of yourself. A good example is the practice of Sufis, a mystical group within Islam, called "whirling." Originating within the Sufi order founded by the Persian poet Jalal-ud-Din Rumi (1207–1273), the movement is performed by *dervishes,* for whom the dance is intended to be a "doorway" between two worlds. Rumi's twentieth-century disciple Suleyman Dede describes the purpose of the practice:

> If you are quiet and in a state of prayer when you Turn, offering everything of yourself to God, then when your body is spinning, there is a completely still point in the center. . . . We do not Turn for ourselves. We turn around in the way we do so that the Light of God may descend upon the earth. As you act as a conduit in the Turn, the light comes through the right hand, and the left hand brings it into this world. . . . We turn for God and for the world, and it is the most beautiful thing you can imagine.[22]

It is indeed beautiful, but it is difficult. I am in awe of the white-clad dervishes who can continue whirling long after most of us would be reeling, dizzy as drunkards. I tried it once, after a short tutorial by an American follower of Rumi who had practiced the discipline for a number of years. My friend taught me to stretch my right arm out to my side at shoulder height with palm upward to receive the energy of God, and to let the left arm, palm down, fall slightly downward as I twirled counterclockwise, in order to become a channel of that energy to the world around me. I was told to keep my gaze on my right hand, rather than "spotting" a point in the room, the way I am accustomed to doing in dance. Later she herself, garbed in white, whirled in a Christian liturgy, and it felt entirely appropriate, a prayer to the God called by T. S. Eliot the "still point of the turning world."

One way we can imitate the action of dervishes is to use flowing cloth or scarves. I will often bring out a bag full of silk scarves at the end of a workshop and invite participants to dance with them, letting the scarf's movement lead them. Inhibitions disappear when it is the scarf that is dancing rather than the person, who might feel inadequate or clumsy. I put on music (like the Randall Thompson "Alleluia," for example) and we just dance, without any agenda. I think that this must have been the way David danced with joy before the Ark of the Covenant. It is certainly the way children dance when they are so full of the music they hear that they cannot help but move.

I suggest that you take a scarf, put on some of your favorite music, and try this yourself. It is pure play—a word that is, of course, suggestively close to another word, pray. It is contemplative. It is beyond words, a celebration of bodily life. It is, in fact, ecstasy!

REFLECTIVE PRAYER

The purpose of reflective prayer is not to empty the mind but to use it, with all its faculties of memory, imagination, and will. Most religions of the world have produced sacred writings to engage the mind, and pondering them in this way has long been considered a way to God. Devout Jews study the Torah, the first five books of the Hebrew Bible; Muslims reverence the Koran; and Christians meditate on both Hebrew and Christian Scriptures. An early founder of communal monasticism, Benedict of Nursia, recommended four hours a day of nourishing the mind with Scripture in this way. He called it *lectio divina*—divine reading. Ignatius Loyola later devised a method of systematic meditation on Scripture called, like this book, *Spiritual Exercises.* He advised the members of his newly formed religious order to take time with Scripture, first reading it, then using all their senses—hearing, taste, touch, and smell, as well as sight—to try to place themselves within the story. They were then to let the story speak to them, listening for what God might be saying to them during this time of prayer. Finally, they were to ask the question, "How can I respond to this message through my outward life?"

About twenty-five years ago, I discovered the impact of adding the kinetic sense to the other five senses while meditating on Scripture. It happened during a sacred dance workshop at a "Clown, Mime, Puppetry and Dance Ministries" conference, which focused on the use of the arts in worship and pastoral work. Our group consisted of several women and one tall Jesuit priest. Our task was to meditate on the story in John 11 of Jesus raising Lazarus, the brother of Mary and Martha, from the tomb. We were then to devise a way to express the story through movement. As we discussed the roles each would play, the Jesuit was the unanimous choice for Jesus—although today we might well have chosen one of the women! I was elected to be Lazarus because I had some dance training. "But I just lie there!" I objected.

Not so! We moved through the story, with the weeping sisters Mary and Martha reaching out beseeching arms, pleading with Jesus to go to Lazarus's tomb, where the mourning bystanders rocked back and forth, heavy with grief. As I waited, recumbent on the floor, my own body became heavier and heavier. It began to dawn on me that I was representing a corpse—that I was dead. I began to wonder how I would feel when the day finally came when this was not just play-acting.

Then, through half-closed eyes, I saw a figure towering over me, and strong gestures beckoning me to stand up. I did not actually hear the command "Lazarus, come forth!" but there was no doubt I had to emerge from my torpor. Slowly, I began to be aware of my body once again and, with difficulty, rose to a sitting position, then to my knees, and finally struggled to my feet. The bystanders encircled me, as if freeing me from the gravecloths. As energy finally surged through my limbs, I gradually came to life. Henry Colman has written a poem about that moment:

> Where am I, or how came I here, hath death
> Bereaved me of my breath,
> Or do I dream?
> Nor can that be, for sure I am
> These are no ensigns of a living man. . . .
> And well remember I,
> My friends on either hand
> Did weeping stand
> To see me die;
> Most certain then it is my soul was fled
> Forth of my clay, and I am buried. . . .
> Was't my Redeemer called, no marvel then
> Though dead, I live again,
> His word alone
> Can raise a soul, though dead in sin,
> Ready the grave of hell to tumble in.[23]

Ever since, I have never heard that story from John without remembering myself as Lazarus. My body had experienced the process of moving from death into new life, not merely in my imagination, but in motion.

We presented our movement meditation at a Quaker-style service afterward, and the conferees who watched were as moved as we who presented it. Onlookers as well as participants related to our enacted story with their bodies, because their kinetic sense was activated like our own. We moved because our brains had sent messages through our neurological systems to our muscles. The onlookers who watched us received the same messages—from brain to neurological system—but the messages did not complete their journey into actual motion. This vicarious yet immobile participation in movement is very likely the reason that ballet audiences flock to see *Swan Lake* or *Firebird* or baseball fans gather at a stadium. We are energized by athletic dancing or fine ball playing, not merely emotionally, but physically.

My colleague Lee and I enacted the Stations of the Cross at Holy Cross Monastery one Good Friday. The stations, each one depicting an event of Good Friday leading up to the crucifixion, line the wall of a long corridor leading to the monastery chapel. As the community moved from station to station, they could see us at the end of the corridor in a pose that interpreted the station. I took many roles—Pontius Pilate, Mary Magdalene, Veronica, and Mary the Mother of Jesus—but Lee represented the central figure of Jesus throughout. Once all were in the chapel, we improvised a dance linking the stations. After the service, one of the monks exclaimed, "Now I know why the Incarnation was necessary!" Seeing a three-dimensional, physical version of the carved plaques on the cloister wall grounded the story of Good Friday in real human life.

In the church in which I grew up, the youth group presented a similar movement prayer called the Mime, in which there were many players depicting the events of Good Friday in slow motion set to music. It begins with Pilate washing his hands so that the blood of Jesus will not be on his conscience, then raising his hand to heaven and slowly lowering it to point at the figure of Jesus. Jesus is given his cross, and falls three times, each time a deeper fall. Veronica wipes Jesus' face, and Mary Magdalene and Jesus' mother Mary kneel at his feet for a blessing. Jesus is "nailed" to the cross by Roman solders, and the blows have never failed to make me flinch. He blesses his disciple John and gives Mary into his care. At the end of his agony he dies and is taken down from the cross and placed in the arms of his mother, a living Pietà. The year my brother played the role of Jesus, I fled sobbing to the privacy of the churchyard afterward.

At our church in Ohio, a small group of parishioners and I have interpreted other Bible stories. On Pentecost (often called the "birthday of the church"), the day when Christians celebrate the coming of the Holy Spirit to the disciples after the ascension of Jesus, a few people rose from the choir stalls and pews as the reading began: "the disciples were all together in one place." As they huddled fearfully in the middle of the chancel, the words "suddenly a sound came from heaven like the rush of a mighty wind" were read, and two of us ran down the side aisles. Behind one of us streamed a length of blue silk-like material, signifying the wind, and behind the other, red material flowed like fire. Once we arrived in the chancel, the "disciples" leapt up and ran out into the congregation throwing to the people in the pews red crepe paper streamers signifying the Spirit. It was not really a performance: it was a "happening" that will long be with us when we hear that story each year.

Once you begin to read Scripture in terms of movement, the possibilities are limitless. One Easter Vigil, I found myself lying in the center of the chancel as one of the dismembered skeletons soon to be brought to life by the prophesying of Ezekiel, who called on God to breathe life into these dry bones. Enacting scenes like this gives new meaning to "fleshing out" the story.

The examples I have given have involved group enactment of Scripture, but "moving the Bible" can be a powerful exercise in your personal prayer as well. Here is one example of an exercise you can do by yourself in your regular time of prayer.

Begin by reading aloud to yourself the story of the Stilling of the Storm, from Mark 4:35–41 (or Matthew 8:23–27 or Luke 8:22–25). Then enact the story. Begin by climbing into a small boat in shallow water. Actually climb in as if you were trying to keeping your balance as you get in. Realize that it can be a challenge to place your weight as close to the center of the boat as possible, as it is not stable, especially when a storm is brewing. In the story, you are worn out after a long day, and you crave some sleep on this voyage. How does it feel when the storm arises? What is the motion of the boat as you begin to wake up? Is your body huddled in fear, as you brace yourself against the force of the waves slapping the boat?

Then become the storm itself. Let the flinging out of your arms mirror the motions of the wind and the waves, as if you were churning up the whole room. What emotions wash over you? How does it feel to let the storm vent its fury through your body? Are you afraid?

"Peace! Be still!" The storm ends. Breathe, and notice your weight. Notice the pace of your heartbeat slowing, and your muscles relaxing. Become, yourself, the "great calm" at the end of the story.

After you have finished this private "movement meditation," take some time to reflect on it. I have found that placing myself right inside this story with my body can uncover hidden fears, and reassures me of the calm that can be God's gift in the midst of chaos. But perhaps it is saying something different to you. Take time to sit quietly with it, in order to discover its power.

There are many stories in the Bible that might lend themselves to this kind of lively reflection. In the Christian Scriptures of the New Testament, for example, you might choose the healing of the blind man Bartimaeus (Mark 10:46–52) or of the cripple or "bent woman" in Luke 13:10–17. Moving through a healing story helps us claim our own need for healing in both body and spirit. Or you might experiment with how it feels to fret like the harassed Martha, bustling about in the kitchen, in contrast to breathing the wisdom and peace of God like Martha's sister Mary, sitting at Jesus' feet in Luke 10:38–42.

In the Hebrew Scriptures there is a powerful story in the third chapter of Genesis, close to the very beginning of the Bible. Moving through the story of Adam and Eve and their expulsion from the Garden of Eden can be an effective way to find good company and new wisdom amidst our own complex transitions and losses. Or how about the well-known story of Jonah and the whale, in which the prophet Jonah, after hearing God's call to sail to confront the citizens of Nineveh, begins by traveling in the opposite direction?

Like the early parts of the Hebrew Scriptures that contain so much legend and drama, some of the later books, such as Job, Daniel, or Esther, also contain colorful tales. The gospels, of course, are full of good stories: stories about Jesus, and the stories that Jesus told. For those who, like most of us, do not know the Bible from cover to cover, it may be frustrating to try to find these stories and others like them among the more than two thousand pages of an ordinary Bible, but I offer two hints. You can borrow a "children's Bible," which usually contains the most action-packed stories from Scripture, and take note of where they occur in an "adult" Bible. It is also helpful to know that most adult Bibles have a summary of the contents of each page either at the top or bottom of the page.

Moving the *themes* underlying the Bible stories is another way to use these texts. Take, for example, the theme of captivity and release. Most of us know the story of Moses in the first chapters of Exodus. The Israelites were slaves of the Egyptian Pharaoh: "The Egyptians...made their lives bitter with hard service in mortar and brick and in every kind of field labor. They were ruthless in all the tasks that they imposed on them" (Exodus 1:13–14). Responding to God's voice calling him from out of the burning bush, Moses led the Israelites over the Red Sea, toward freedom and the Promised Land.

This passage from bondage to freedom is a recurring theme, not only in biblical history, but in our personal lives, and it can be illuminating to contrast these two states of being.

How would your body feel if it were bound? How would you move if you were in chains? Are there any situations in which your psyche feels this way?

Now, what does freedom feel like? Do you feel the release of heaviness and tension?

Are there things in your life that actually have the effect of bondage, tying you up or weighing you down and keeping you from living as "the glory of God— the human being fully alive"? The "chains" may be such things as addictions to overwork, alcohol, or food that affect your relationships and your health. They may be unreasonable expectations on the part of others, or even your own expectations of yourself. Perhaps they are resentments that you carry with you from long ago. Sometimes "acting out" the passage from captivity to freedom can be like a dress rehearsal for actually casting off our bonds.

Other pairs of contrasted themes, such as exile and return or despair and hope, can become the content for reflection through movement. How does it feel to be far away from your "home," disconnected either from your familiar environment or that interior place in your spirit where you feel "at home" with yourself? How does hopelessness feel, and what happens in your body when it is reenergized by recognizing the promise of the future?

Our dreams often provide rich content for reflection through movement. When you have had a powerful dream, you might begin to plumb its depths by moving the way the various parts of the dream make you feel. After we put our former house on the market fifteen years ago, we were in a quandary when a very demanding and difficult young couple made an offer. We had loved our home, and wanted the next occupants to be people to whom we felt a good connection. However, we needed to sell it in order to move to our new life five hundred miles away. During the critical weekend in which we had to decide whether to accept the offer, I had a dream that solved the problem for me. I was in a bus going up a steep hill and recognized one of the occupants, a friend who had (in real life) died the year before. The bus stalled, and most of us got out in order to continue the journey on foot. My friend did not, but remained in her seat. We looked in horror as the brakes gave way and the bus rolled backward down the hill, to disappear into a deep body of water at the bottom. I thought, "If I had stayed on that bus, I would have died."

When I awoke, the movement in the dream had freed me to accept the couple's offer. If I had had any doubts, I could have enacted the dream in a movement reflection. But it was perfectly clear. If I had remained in the bus, I would have rolled backward down the hill with my friend whose life was in the past. I couldn't cling to that house in which I had made an important part of life's journey that was now finished. Instead, I had to move on, taking the next steps in our life. My husband agreed, and we called the real estate broker to tell her our decision.

When we use our bodies in reflecting upon Scripture, themes, or dreams, we are drawing on a kind of wisdom that is different from our usual linear thought. I remember the Episcopal priest and writer Tilden Edwards saying during a workshop when I was in seminary, "When you have a decision to make, and there is a conflict between the head and the gut, choose the gut." How do I know how I really feel? It is the "gut," or body, that tells me. Anyone who has worried about a family member who has not returned home at the expected time will recognize the uncomfortable feeling in the pit of the stomach, as the imagination begins to run riot—and then the feeling of "breathing easier" when the car is heard in the driveway. When we enact a Bible story as the bodyspirits that we are, we are no longer spectators, but draw closer to being participants. When we struggle with personal decisions and conflicts, we can also draw on this body-wisdom, which helps us to connect intellect, emotion, and our physical reality, as we try to follow God's call to us throughout our lives.

✳

VERBAL PRAYER

Verbal prayer is prayer with words. The words can be psalms from the Hebrew Scriptures, prayers from a prayer book, hymn texts, songs, poems, or our own spontaneous utterances. Many people find that words provide a kind of "anchor" for their attentiveness to God. Some recite the Daily Office, consisting of set prayers, psalms, and lessons said at morning and in the evening, and sometimes at noon and for Compline (the last prayers said at night) as well. Others use prayers such as the Lord's Prayer or other prayers from a prayer book during their daily prayer time. They find that the familiarity of the words provides a structure within which their spirit can grow. However, the problem with verbal prayer, which includes the prayers we say and hear so often in our public worship, is that after we have prayed them for years, the time may come when they are so familiar that we are in danger of saying them by rote. We might "come to" in the middle of a prayer only to find that our minds and hearts are far away.

An embarrassing example of such a wandering mind once happened to me, not actually because of over-familiarity, but because of absentmindedness. It took place when I was an inexperienced priest, during one of my first celebrations of the Eucharist. My mind wandered from the task at hand, and suddenly I found myself beginning the prayer of consecration without remembering whether or not I had led the congregation in the *Sanctus*: "Holy, holy, holy...." I had not. Afterward, I asked another priest whether he had noticed. To my relief, he replied, "I just thought my mind had wandered," and, because he is such an honest soul, I do not think the response was merely out of kindness. I received similar responses from several of my classmates. The words of the liturgy can just wash over us, comfortingly familiar— sometimes too familiar. Ever since, I have tried harder to practice the counsel of the monk who tutored me before my first Eucharist: "The most important thing about leading liturgy is to *pray* it."

Perhaps you have a book of prayers that you use daily, and the same thing has happened to you. It is one reason I welcome new translations of the Psalms. More than once, in saying them I have wandered mentally and then "come to" the way I did in that Eucharist. This certainly can happen easily in a psalm as familiar as Psalm 23, "The Lord is my shepherd, I shall not be in want." To give it new freshness, try the following exercise. It is based on the fact that the words on our lips are expressions of feelings and thoughts that have preceded the words. The words are merely the end result of another, nonverbal way of thinking. In order to find new meaning in old words, we need to go behind them, or beyond them, to the deep source from which they sprang. This can be done above all through movement. There is no right or wrong way to do this. The point is to try to convey the *feeling* that is the source of the words, in any way that you are moved to do so.

Here is an example of a way to communicate Psalm 23, although I urge you eventually to create your own movements.

> *The LORD is my shepherd;*
>   *I shall not be in want.*
> *He makes me lie down in green pastures*
>   *and leads me beside still waters.*
> *He revives my soul*
>   *and guides me along right pathways for his Name's sake.*
> *Though I walk through the valley of the shadow of death,*
> *I shall fear no evil;*
>   *for you are with me;*
>   *your rod and your staff, they comfort me.*
> *You spread a table before me in the presence of those who trouble me;*
>   *you have anointed my head with oil,*
>   *and my cup is running over.*
> *Surely your goodness and mercy shall follow me all the days of my life;*
>   *and I will dwell in the house of the LORD for ever. (King James Version)*

Imagine that you need to communicate the sense of this psalm to someone who is unable to hear. You can choose from one of two points of view: the one watched over by the shepherd, and the shepherd.

If you choose the first, you might try to express the sense of being protected by a divine shepherd by looking upward, reaching toward the sky with your arms, then cupping your hands in front of you to welcome the gifts that God gives you. Next, you might bend very low and even kneel on the ground, and then rise slowly, as if a strong hand is helping you to rise and walk. As you enter dangerous territory, you may first move tentatively, trembling and timid, looking in all directions, until you feel God's gift of courage coming into your body and you walk forward firmly. Finally, you can touch your head and forehead, as a sign that God anoints your head with oil, and then lift your cupped hands to your lips to drink the overflowing cup of God's love.

Since it is said we are made in the image of God, you can, without fear of blasphemy, choose to enact the role of the *shepherd* instead! The flock, of course, is really the human race. What motions would you make in serving and protecting God's other children? What movements would you use to suggest bestowing upon them the human equivalent of green pastures and still waters? How would you restore the souls of others through gestures of healing and compassion? How would you lead others in God's pathway of peace and justice? What gestures indicate that you wish to defend others from the evil that is a part of the world's reality? What movements would you use to affirm the sacredness, or anointing, of each human life? As the shepherd, you are representing goodness and mercy. How is that reflected in your bearing, in the expansiveness of your movements, and in your facial expression?

If you wish, you can add music to this movement meditation. For this psalm, I have often depended on those compositions of Bach that have a gentle pastoral rhythm, such as his Concerto in D minor for two violins or the slow movement of one of his oboe concertos. Finally, you may even wish to repeat the movements to the music you have chosen, without thinking of the words of the psalm.

Even more familiar than Psalm 23 is the Lord's Prayer. You can, of course, invent your own movements. The following is a suggestion that may serve as a catalyst for you to discover your own way of making the prayer more meaningful by expressing it through your body.

Begin by standing, with the arms at the sides. Then, as you say "Our Father," begin to raise the arms slowly until they are stretched toward the sky, and look upward.

When you say "Give us this day our daily bread," bring down your hands, reaching in front of you with the palms up in a receptive position.

At "Forgive us our trespasses," cross the arms over the chest in an "x," and bow your head.

Reach out to each side as if you were taking the hands of neighbors as you say "as we forgive those who trespass against us," looking to each side as you do so.

Bow deeply at the words, "and lead us not into temptation, but deliver us from evil."

At "for thine is the kingdom," raise the arms once again and look upward.

While body-prayer helps us to discover new meaning in prayers that we are tempted to say merely by rote, it also helps us to delve into the meaning of less familiar texts. I have on my shelves books of prayers for peace, for the natural environment, and for various seasons of the year. I have books from Iona, Taizé, and New Zealand, and collections that include prayers from many of the world's great religions. Using prayers from other cultures and faith traditions, you can pray with people who may understand God in ways different from your own, giving you perspective on your own faith, or perhaps articulating something you believe but for which you have not yet found words.

The following prayer, for example, was written by the fifteenth-century Indian mystic Kabir, who is claimed both by Hindus and by Muslims. It reminds me of the sheer joy of life.

Dance, my heart! dance to-day with joy.
The strains of love fill the days and nights with music,
  and the world is listening to its melodies:
Mad with joy, life and death dance to the rhythm of this music.
The hills and the sea and the earth dance.
The world of man dances in laughter and tears.
Why put on the robe of the monk, and live aloof from the
  world in lonely pride?
Behold! My heart danceth in the delight of a hundred arts;
  and the Creator is well pleased.[24]

Try inventing your own movements to this prayer. Some ideas might be to begin by clapping a rhythm—perhaps one like "slow, slow, quick-quick," or a skipping pattern like "slow, fast-slow, fast-slow"—close to your heart, expanding the rebound until they are very large movements. Then begin to move to the rhythm, as you cup your hand to your ears, to "listening to [the] melodies" of the world.

Continuing the rhythm, suggest the hills, sea, and earth by tracing with your hands the shape of a hill, then the movement of waves, and finally use your weight to stamp more forcefully, to represent "earth." Suggest the laughter and tears through both movements indicating happiness and sorrow, as well as your facial expressions.

Suddenly, when you arrive at the line that begins "Why put on the robe of the monk," cease the rhythm and walk slowly and solemnly.

Just as suddenly, when you arrive at the final line, "Behold!", begin the rhythm again with both feet and hands, moving with joy around the space.

Alternatively, you can choose some music that, for you, expresses the joyous spirit of this prayer, and move to it.

Another resource for verbal movement prayer is poetry, that artful distillation of reality that can so greatly illuminate our spirits. If you have poems that especially speak to you, you can enter into their meaning more profoundly if you let your whole body "read" them. One of Martha Graham's best-known works is just such a meditation, called "Letter to the World," inspired by the life and poetry of Emily Dickinson.

I have always loved hymns; their texts for me are windows into the lives and prayer of my spiritual ancestors.[25] Especially when the words are accompanied by music, they are a rich resource for movement. Many religious publishers produce recordings of hymns that can accompany this kind of verbal body-prayer.

I once led an intergenerational workshop for Advent based on "O come, O come, Emmanuel," where we explored the wonderful poetry of the ancient "O" antiphons on which this hymn is based. The "O" antiphons are short verses that are still used before and after the *Magnificat* in some churches, convents, and monasteries between December 16 and 23. They can be understood as various ways of naming the attributes of the anticipated Messiah: Wisdom, Adonai, Root of Jesse, Key of David, Dayspring, King of nations, Emmanuel. The children particularly enjoyed "O Wisdom," in which they were asked to create chaos in the beginning until Wisdom, impersonated by one of the parents, gently moved them into an orderly pattern. In "O Key of David," they huddled in a "prison" made from the interlocking arms of the adults in attendance, until the "Key" came and unlocked them. With their parents and teachers, they created an enormous Jesse tree, each person connecting a hand or foot with another person's hand or foot so that the intertwining bodies practically filled the room. Finally, we cradled "Emmanuel" as an infant in our arms. I hope that these children, now grown, still remember the wonder of God's presence with us as that child, as well as the promise of God's order over chaos and the gift of freedom from the things that bind us.[26] Individuals also can also pray these poetic antiphons suggesting some of the attributes of the divine, through imaginatively interpreting them in movement.

Perhaps the most popular "hymn dance" I teach has been reconstructed by dance historians as an example of the way the members of Shaker sect—so named because of their ecstatic shaking "movement prayer"—might have danced their well-known hymn, "Simple Gifts." It is set to a catchy nineteenth-century tune made popular by Aaron Copland's *Appalachian Spring*.

'Tis the gift to be simple, 'tis the gift to be free
Take four steps forward, with the arms in front of you and the hands, cupped with palms upward, making two small scooping motions with each step. (Shakers believed that this movement helped to gather blessings.)

'Tis the gift to come down where we ought to be
Take four steps backward to where you began, shaking the arms in front of you loosely with palms downward, twice with each step. (Shakers believed that this movement "shook off" the negative things in their lives—and many people can testify to the fact that it does help!)

And when we find ourselves in the place just right,
'Twill be in the valley of love and delight.
Repeat the above movements.

When true simplicity is gained
Step sideways to the right on the right foot, opening the arms to the side with elbows bent and palms facing one another. Then bring the left foot beside the

right, as you also bring the hands together, with palms together in a position of prayer, and bow your body forward.

Then reverse the movement, step sideways to the left on the left foot, bringing the right foot beside it, and bowing.

To bow and to bend we shan't be ashamed
Repeat the above movements. (For my purposes, I like to think of "simplicity" not only as outward simplicity of life, but as mindfulness of our true center in God. When we act from that center, we do not need to remain stiff and unyielding, but can be free to bow and to bend, open and resilient in our dealings with others.)

To turn, turn, will be our delight
Turn around in a small circle to the right (clockwise), as if you were walking around a pie plate, with the arms lifted up to the sides, the elbows bent, and the hands about shoulder height, with palms facing.

Till by turning, turning we come round right.
Repeat a similar circle, turning toward the left (counterclockwise). (In fact, when we are "grounded" in God, we can even be free enough to change, perhaps even turning full circle!)

This hymn can be danced by a group as well as by an individual. The Shakers would have performed this dance in two lines, with the men on one side of the room and the women on the other side. Now, because the ratio of men to women in a gathering is rarely balanced, it works best danced in a circle.

Do you have particular hymn texts or prayers that speak to you? Perhaps it is the lovely hymn "Morning Has Broken," which you can interpret by picking up two dawn-colored scarves from the floor and letting them dance in the air to fill the space with "praise for the morning, fresh from the Word."

Or perhaps you love the prayer of St. Francis:

Lord, make us instruments of your peace. Where there is hatred, let us sow love; where there is injury, pardon; where there is discord, union; where there is doubt, faith; where there is despair, hope; where there is darkness, light; where there is sadness, joy. Grant that we may not so much seek to be consoled as to console; to be understood as to understand; to be loved as to love. For it is in giving that we receive; it is in pardoning that we are pardoned; and it is in dying that we are born to eternal life.[27]

Try moving this prayer, with its great contrasts that are so perfectly suited to interpretation through the body. When you improvise the qualities and actions of the peacemaker, you are likely to become more and more transformed into an instrument of peace yourself: a bodyspirit in whom the life and presence of God dwells.

CHAPTER 4

REST

ALTHOUGH I AM by nature a contemplative, with a need for solitude and quiet, I also take great pleasure in being with other people, working and doing. Not only am I energized by activity, but encoded in my genetic makeup is the work ethic of my forebears. I resist taking naps, and "wasting time" seems tinged with immorality. And yet I know so well the importance of "wasting time" with God! I encourage in myself, and in others, the "activity" of resting in God's presence, in touch with our truest selves and open to the beauty of the world around us. In order to allow myself to savor such time, I need frequent reminders of its value by poets like Charles Péguy, in whose poem "Abandonment" God speaks of the human being with affection, tinged by a little exasperation:

> A funny creature...
> You can still ask a lot of him. He is not too bad....
> But what you can't ask of him, by gum, is a little hope,
> A little confidence, don't you know, a little relaxation.
> A little yielding, a little abandonment into my hands,
> A little giving in.

God eventually speaks to the night, asking it to bestow the gift of sleep on this rest-less and driven creature:

> Let him stretch out his poor weary limbs on a bed of rest.
> Let him ease his aching heart a little on a bed of rest.
> Above all, let his head stop working....
> Let his thoughts stop moving about and struggling
> inside his head and rattling like calabash seeds.[28]

I am also reminded of the value of rest by theologians like Abraham Heschel in his book *The Sabbath* and Tilden Edwards in *Sabbath Time*. While Heschel's book deals with the actual Sabbath observance of practicing Jews, Edwards expands the concept of sabbath-keeping for Christians. For both, observing sabbath time is an integral part of spirituality.

Heschel speaks of the Sabbath as "a sanctuary in time," where we can experience rest and delight. It is "more than an armistice, more than an interlude; it is a profound conscious harmony of man and the world, a sympathy for all things and a participa-tion in the spirit that unites what is below and what is above.... This is Sabbath, and the true happiness of the universe." Then he addresses those of us for whom work never seems to be finished: "'Six days shalt thou labor and do all thy work' (Exodus 20:8). Is it possible for a human being to do all his work in six days? Does not our work always remain incomplete? What the verse means to convey is: Rest on the Sabbath as if all your work were done."[29]

For his part, Edwards uses the word "sabbath time" to describe not only obser-vance of a special day of rest during the week, but a special quality of time that we can enter daily. This time is like an "incubator for nourishing our being in the image of God, in ways that overflow into appropriate care for the world."[30] In other words, rest transforms both our sense of ourselves in relationship to God and the quality of our subsequent activity.

Sabbath living has to do both with taking time for prayer, rest, and delight, and with the pace of life. When I was a college student in the midwest and returned to the New York metropolitan area for holidays, I used to think I had entered a film that was being shown on a projector that was set to the wrong speed: too fast! Today, when we visit the east coast, my husband and I still experience that acceleration, beginning with the behavior of the traffic as Route 80 crosses New Jersey and draws nearer to the George Washington Bridge. The fast pace is contagious; it is difficult not to march—or rather, run—to the same drummer as the people around us. But remember that Buddhist priest with whom I opened this book, walking meditatively across town, and the envious glances of the passers-by!

It is one thing to move quickly in order to get things done, and quite another to get caught in a rhythm that is destructive to our well-being. Our best way of not confusing the two is to become more conscious of our bodies. Are you revitalized by the excitement of doing what you are doing at the pace you are doing it? Or do you feel worn out by this pace you set for yourself, as if it were driving you? If the latter is true, there are two things you can do. One is to give serious consideration to changing your schedule or your lifestyle, over a period of weeks or months. The other, more immediate solution is to take a moment of sabbath time for conscious relaxation. If we notice those moments when our muscles begin to tighten and our breathing and heartbeat begin to quicken, we can respond to these signals by taking a deep breath and consciously relaxing our muscles.

✳

RELAXATION

The following exercise will help us learn to recognize the signals that we need some sabbath time, and will also help us to take time out from our "fast forward" mode of life in order to relax and rest.

This exercise is best done while lying down. You can also do it in a chair that will support your body as you relax. If you are lying down on the floor, you can either stretch out your legs, or lie in a "constructive rest" position.

There are two versions of this latter pose. In one, you bend your knees and place your feet flat on the floor, letting your knees come together if that helps you better relax your leg muscles. In the second, your legs are bent at the knee, and the calves and the feet rest on the seat of a chair. There should be a right angle at the hip joint and another one at the knee. This position also reverses the pull of gravity on the circulatory and lymphatic systems, further relaxing the body.

First, notice your weight on the floor. Let all the muscles go. You may need to tense each muscle first, or to move it first, to find where the tension is being held, then release it. Or perhaps just a mental suggestion will do the trick.

Send the message "let go" to each muscle group in turn, beginning with the feet. Relax the right foot, the right calf, the right thigh. Relax the left foot, the left calf, the left thigh. Relax the buttocks.

Relax the abdomen, the ribcage, the chest. Relax the muscles of the back, and imagine you feel the tension just draining from the spine.

Relax the tight trapezius muscles between the shoulders. Relax the right shoulder, the right upper arm, the right forearm, and the right hand. Relax the left shoulder, the left upper arm, the left forearm, and the left hand.

Relax the back of the neck and the front of the neck. Relax the jaw, the cheeks, the area around the eyes, the area between the eyebrows, the forehead, and the scalp.

Picture the inner organs relaxing. Notice that your breath is slower and shallower. Scan the body again, beginning at the feet. Is any tension left? If so, gently release it.

Calm your mind as well by using a word or an image of peace. You might mentally repeat the word "rest" or "shalom." Or picture a place where you have felt profoundly peaceful and able to relax, perhaps lying on a beach, praying in a chapel, or sitting in a rocking chair looking out over the mountains.

Believe it or not, this position of profound rest is a form of body prayer. Through rest, the body reminds you that you can trust God to take care of things for a while. You are allowing your busy, overworked self to take a sabbatical. For a while at least, you are able to let go of controlling things; you are "letting go and letting God."

This kind of rest is profoundly rejuvenating, often even more so than sleep. Physiologists tell us that we have entered a *hypometabolic* state, in which our metabolism slows down. It is just the opposite from the "fight or flight" response that can make us hurried, harried, and stressed. The fight or flight response served our distant ancestors well, sending the adrenaline coursing through their bodies should it became necessary to wrestle with an adversary or run from a predator. It is usually unwise to fight or flee when we encounter a difficult situation at the office or at home, but our body—not yet programmed to ignore threats—sends the messages anyway. Eventually these aborted responses begin to take their toll on our health. The observance of deliberate sabbath times is not only prescribed by many medical practitioners now, but has long been a recommended spiritual practice for people of faith. In my opinion, it should also be required discipline for the leaders of the nations!

✳

MASSAGE

I had my first massage a little over five years ago, after years of reluctance to subject myself to the hands of a stranger. The masseur was a skilled practitioner whose training had included both Swedish massage and therapeutic massage for sports injuries. His thorough knowledge of the musculature of the body, and his sensitivity to the needs of each muscle, soon put me at my ease. I relaxed and became, you might say, putty in his hands! As he worked on me, in fact, it was just that image that came to me: the picture of God molding the first human being in Genesis 2:7—the Hebrew creation story. Just as I had once experienced what it must have been like to be Lazarus when I danced the story of Jesus raising Lazarus from the tomb, I now experienced how it could have felt to be molded from earth by God the sculptor.

Like many people, I have a mild sideways curvature or scoliosis in my back, and massage helps to align it: the crooked is made straight. When I first stand and walk after a massage, I feel like the newly oiled tin woodsman in *The Wizard of Oz*. I feel cleansed as well, with the accumulated tensions in my muscles literally squeezed out of me. This is no figment of my imagination: what has happened is that the hands of the masseur cause the muscles to release the deposits of lactic acid that build up within them during the course of daily life. For this reason, a massage client is always told to drink lots of water after a session, to flush these acids out of the body.

I rise from the massage table with gratitude for the gift of another human being whose skilled hands have cared for me. Giving massages is certainly love made tangible. Like the intercessions of others when I am in need of them, a massage reminds me that sometimes I just cannot accomplish alone what another can do for me.

RHYTHM

Sometimes the need for rest is really a need for change. Physical trainers advise us that even if a form of exercise is good in itself, we may harm ourselves if we do too much of it. A common example is the deteriorating knee joints of people who have run every day for years, especially on hard surfaces like asphalt or cement. Strength training is another example: we are advised to rest the muscles for a day before another session.

I find that I need other kinds of rest as well. As I was finishing this manuscript, I was also preparing for a conference. My days were chock-full of putting together words that were supposed to carry weight in order to reach out to my readers and conference participants. It was not physical rest I needed; I wanted something *lightweight*. I found myself, during the week of the conference, longing for a mental rest from this task, important as it was. Serendipitously, when I had packed for the trip I had tucked into my luggage a mystery novel passed on to me by a friend. As soon as my flight home took off, I reached into my carry-on bag and spent the next couple of hours enjoying the exploits of a Scottish policeman. It felt something like the progressive relaxation of a yoga class—for the brain instead of the body!

When I come home from my infrequent shopping trips to the local mall, I need a rest from the noise of the incessant background music in every store that sometimes makes me want to turn around and walk out. Yet I find great pleasure in hearing music I like: after several days of not attending a concert or turning on the radio or CD player, I need to rest from silence. After weeks filled with travel, conferences, and visitors, I need to rest from being in the presence of so many people. When I have been alone for hours in my study, I need to hop on my bicycle and go to town, which is small enough that I inevitably meet friends and acquaintances.

Life today is so stimulating that our senses can be overloaded. It is important to recognize this and to take time to "rest" them by using them in a different way. A good example is the "slow food" movement, in which chefs and diners who like carefully cooked, leisurely meals have organized a campaign to remind people of the alternative to the fast-food chains that are proliferating all over the world.

Perhaps we should initiate campaigns for "slow hearing," "slow looking," "slow touching," and "slow smelling" as well. "Slow hearing" would occur when we set aside time to relax, put on a CD (or go to a concert), and do one thing: listen. When we engage in "slow looking," we would let our eyes dwell on an object or work of art as if it were the only one in the world. When I think of "slow touching," I remember the exercise I used to do with preschoolers, using objects with various textures. Each child would be so totally focused on feeling the softness of a square of velvet or the smoothness of a rock that sometimes they wanted to keep holding it, reluctant to pass it on to another child. "Slow smelling" has already been immortalized in the line "Wake up and smell the roses," which we can change, for our purposes, to "Slow down and smell the roses."

Péguy—and Edwards and Heschel as well—would approve.

CHAPTER 5

NO BODY, BUT YOURS

HAVE YOU EVER been a guest at a lavish buffet where there were so many tempting dishes spread out on the tables, from smoked salmon to chocolate mousse, that you felt challenged to try as many things as possible during that one meal?

This smorgasbord of exercises is *not* like that now-or-never buffet. It is a spread that is always available for you. You can take a helping of one dish for a week or so, and then try another. You can try one kind of exercise each day of the week. You can take a trial class in a particular technique. You can mix and match, on any given day.

Ultimately, a balanced diet should nourish your aerobic fitness, your strength, and your flexibility. Some modes of exercise benefit all three; some accomplish only one. If we only lifted weights, for example, we would become muscle-bound. I am reminded of this when I forget to stretch the quadriceps muscles in my thighs after a long bicycle ride, and then struggle to stretch my leg behind me in ballet class the next day.

What lies behind this smorgasbord is an attitude that is more important than any given mode of exercise. It is the belief that we are children of a loving God who saw all things as good. Because of this, we are motivated to become good stewards of our physical selves. If we truly accept—not only with our intellects but in our "gut"—that God loves us, we can begin to love ourselves as bodyspirit. Care for the body is an expression of that love. From the very beginning of life, we respond to such care. Writer Diane Ackerman, in *A Natural History of the Senses,* tells of working with a tiny infant in a ward for premature babies in a Miami hospital: "Gently, I move his limbs in a mini-exercise routine, stretching out an arm and bending the elbow tight, opening the legs and bending the knees to the chest. Peaceful but alert; he seems to be enjoying it. We turn him onto his tummy once more, and again I begin caressing his head and shoulders. This is the first of three daily touch sessions for him."[31]

This kind of touching and relaxation actually keeps the baby alive. Ackerman tells us that massaged babies gain weight as much as fifty percent faster than unmassaged babies. At the other end of the spectrum, gerontologists suggest that exercise is like a "magic pill" that helps us age well. In any given group of over-fifty-five-year-olds, I can always spot those who exercise, for they seem younger than their chronological contemporaries.

The question is this: how can we choose bodyspirit practices that we will actually continue to incorporate into our life? I have a theory about that. If I were to list three activities from the smorgasbord that give me the most pleasure, they would be bicycling, swimming, and dancing. All of these activities were part of my play when I was a child. Indelible in my memory is the moment my father was able to let go of his hold on my new two-wheeler and I could propel myself up our dead-end street and swoosh around and around the circle at the end. I am wondering if the exhilaration I sometimes feel while cycling is not a part of my body-memory, re-celebrating this new-found independence and freedom.

As for swimming, my mother jokingly called me and my brothers "water-rats," although I would have preferred "mermaid." We played underwater games in a large saltwater pool at the edge of Long Island Sound, but better still was jumping off my father's small sailboat in the middle of the Sound to cool off. I have already written about my childhood joy in dancing. I am sure that the reason I do not find the hard work of a ballet class overly onerous is that I am, in some way, once again a young girl when standing at the barre.

Certain movements also seem embedded in my youth. A couple of the exercises I teach from the Taoist tradition take me back to childhood. One is to stand and swing the arms back and forth, letting the knees bend at the bottom of the swing. The second is to swing the arms, with the hands in a soft fist, around the body, first to the left and then to the right. Taoists call this "knocking at the gate of heaven," but I call it "waiting for the school bus at the corner of our street."

I have not spoken of team sports, but, as I think about what activities will please us enough for us to continue to engage in them, they must not go unmentioned. I am wondering if our degree of introversion or extroversion might come into play here. Is it because I am an introvert that I have usually chosen solitary exercise? Would extroverts be more likely to enjoy softball, racquetball, or tennis? Where does a sport like golf (without the club cars, of course) fit in?

Giving time to keeping our bodyspirit fit and healthy is not self-indulgent. Rather, it is taking the necessary care of the "temples" in which we are living. We can fill those temples with all manner of prayer, including the prayer that our bodies themselves express. Unlike cathedrals and churches, these temples actually move! And they can move in service to others and to the world. That, in the end, is the reason I exercise. I want to be able to serve God and my neighbor as long as I live, to the best of my ability. Teresa of Avila, the great saint and teacher of prayer, put it this way:

> Christ has no body on earth now, but yours;
>   No hands, but yours;
>   No feet, but yours.
> Yours are the eyes through which
>   he is to look out his compassion to the world.
> Yours are the feet with which he is to go about doing good.
> And yours are the hands with which he is to bless us now.

NOTES

1. *The Saint Helena Psalter* (New York: Church Publishing, Inc., 2004). Unless otherwise indicated, all psalm quotations are from the *Saint Helena Psalter*.

2. *The Book of Occasional Services 2003* (New York: Church Publishing, Inc., 2004),151.

3. Donna Farhi, *The Breathing Book* (New York: Henry Holt & Co., 1996), xv.

4. Nancy Roth, *The Breath of God: An Approach to Prayer* (Cambridge, Mass.: Cowley Publications, 1990, 2002).

5. Thich Nhat Hanh, *The Long Road Turns to Joy: A Guide to Walking Meditation* (Berkeley, Calif.: Parallax Press, 1996), 4.

6. *Ibid.,* 36.

7. Helen Curry, *The Way of the Labyrinth* (New York: Penguin, 2000) 210.

8. Nancy Roth, *An Invitation to Christian Yoga* (New York: Church Publishing, Inc., 1989, 2001, 2005).

9. Henri Nouwen, *With Open Hands* (Notre Dame: Ave Maria Press, 1972), 154.

10. Paul Crompton, *The Art of Tai Chi* (Shaftesbury, Dorset, England: Element Books, Ltd., 1993), ix.

11. My thanks to Br. David Vryhof, SSJE, for sharing this information from Colin Turnbull, a cultural anthropologist.

12. Brooke Siler, *The Pilates Body* (New York: Broadway Books, 2000), 8.

13. M. Scott Peck, *The Road Less Traveled* (New York: Simon and Schuster, 1978), 15.

14. Yehudi Menuhin and Curtis W. Davis, *The Music of Man* (New York: Methuen, Inc., 1979), 2–3.

15. Isadora Duncan, *The Art of the Dance* (New York: Theatre Art Books, 1928, 1970), 102–3.

16. Thomas Merton, *The Monastic Journey,* Brother Patrick Hart, ed. (Kansas City: Sheed Andrews and McMeel, Inc., 1977), 17.

17. Sydney Carter, "Lord of the Dance," in *Songs for Liturgy* and *More Hymns and Spiritual Songs* (Fort Lauderdale: Walton Music Corporation, 1971), H–63.

18. Dorothy Sayers, "Why Work?" in *Creed or Chaos* (New York: Harcourt, Brace, and Co., 1949), 57.

19. George Herbert, "The Elixir," in *The Poems of George Herbert* (London: Oxford University Press, 1961), 174.

20. Shunryu Suzuki, *Zen Mind, Beginner's Mind* (New York: Weatherhill, 1973), 26.

21. Jon M. Sweeney, *Praying With Our Hands* (Woodstock, Vt.: Skylight Paths Publishing, 2000), 75.

22. Suleyman Dede, "Why We Turn," in *Lovers of Mevlanda,* vol. 2, no. 4 (Winter, 1997), 5.

23. Henry Colman, "On Lazarus Raised from Death," in Robert Atwan and Laurance Wieder, ed., *Chapters Into Verse* (New York: Oxford University Press, Inc., 2000), 334.

24. Barbara Green and Victor Gollancz, ed., *God of a Hundred Names: Prayers of Many Peoples and Creeds* (London: Victor Gollancz, Lit., 1962), 248–9.

25. See my series of books of meditations on hymn texts, *A Closer Walk; Awake, My Soul!; New Every Morning;* and *Praise My Soul* (New York: Church Publishing, Inc., 1998, 1999, 2000, 2001).

26. More about this, as well as other movement ideas, can be found in *We Sing of God,* Robert and Nancy Roth, ed. (New York: Church Publishing, Inc., 1989).

27. *The Book of Common Prayer* (New York: Church Publishing, Inc., 1977), 833.

28. Charles Péguy, "Abandonment," in *Perfected Steel, Terrible Crystal: an unconventional source book of spiritual readings in poetry and prose,* Ned O'Gorman, ed. (New York: The Seabury Press, 1981), 103–4.

29. Abraham Joshua Heschel, *The Sabbath* (New York: Farrar, Straus and Giroux, 1951), 31–2.

30. Tilden Edwards, *Sabbath Time* (New York: The Seabury Press, 1982), 6.

31. Diane Ackerman, *A Natural History of the Senses* (New York: Vintage Books, 1990), 73.

Printed in the USA
CPSIA information can be obtained
at www.ICGtesting.com
JSHW052018140824
68134JS00027B/2541

9 781596 270053